POINTS OF INTEREST

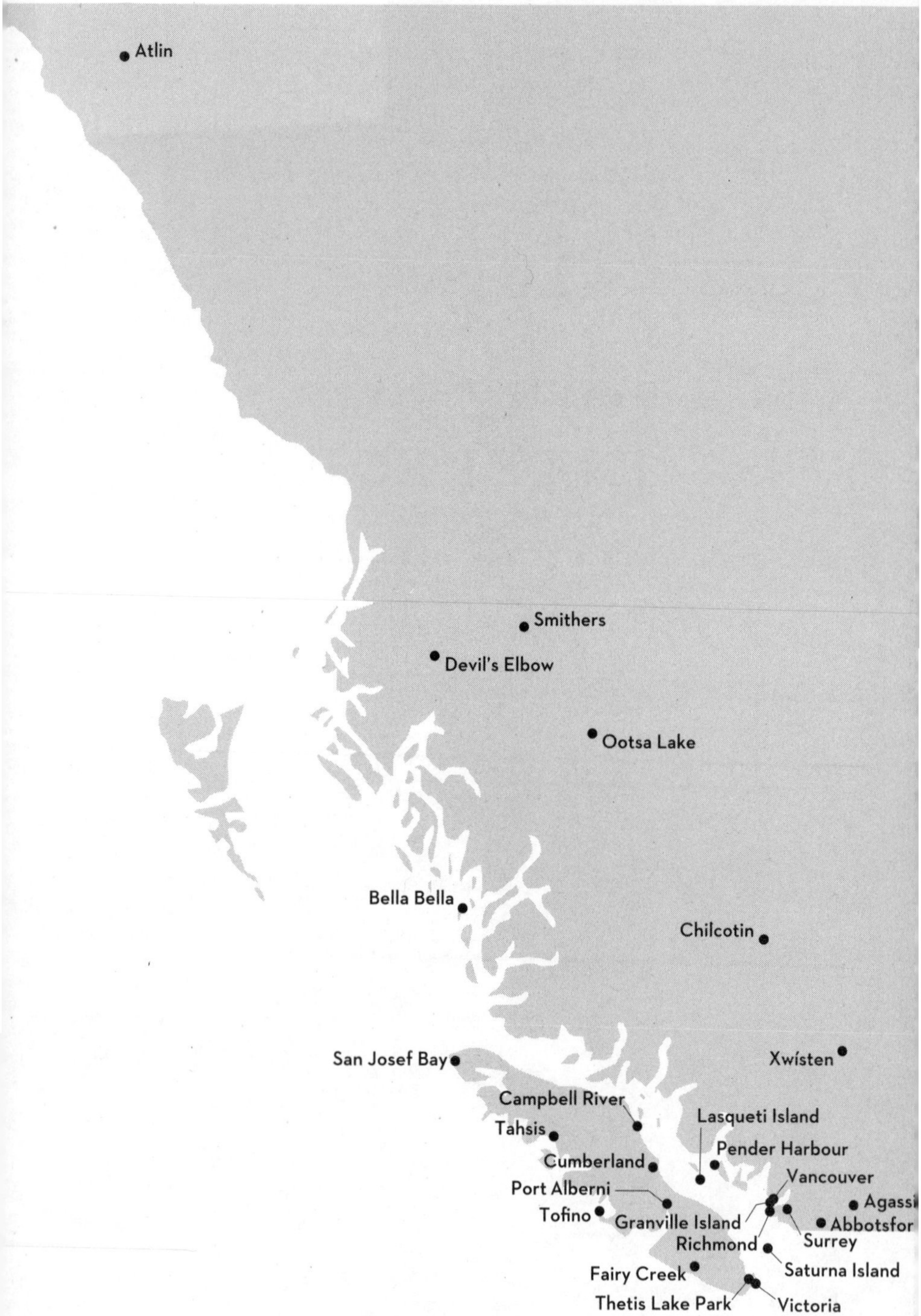

Atlin

Smithers

Devil's Elbow

Ootsa Lake

Bella Bella

Chilcotin

San Josef Bay

Xwísten

Campbell River

Lasqueti Island

Tahsis

Pender Harbour

Cumberland

Vancouver

Port Alberni

Agassi

Tofino

Granville Island

Abbotsfor

Richmond

Surrey

Saturna Island

Fairy Creek

Thetis Lake Park

Victoria

POINTS OF INTEREST

IN SEARCH OF THE PLACES, PEOPLE, AND STORIES OF B.C.

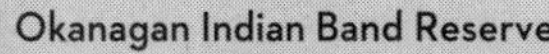

GREYSTONE BOOKS
Vancouver/Berkeley/London

24 25 26 27 28 5 4 3 2 1

Greystone Books Ltd.
greystonebooks.com

Cataloguing data available from Library and Archives Canada
ISBN 978-1-77840-138-1 (pbk.)
ISBN 978-1-77840-139-8 (epub)

Copy editing by Brian Lynch
Proofreading by Rachel Taylor
Design by Jessica Sullivan
Illustrations by Nora Kelly

Printed and bound in Canada on FSC® certified paper at Friesens. The FSC® label means that materials used for the product have been responsibly sourced.

Greystone Books thanks the Canada Council for the Arts, the British Columbia Arts Council, the Province of British Columbia through the Book Publishing Tax Credit, and the Government of Canada for supporting our publishing activities.

Canada

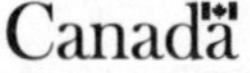

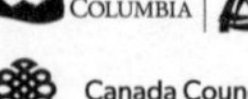

Canada Council for the Arts
Conseil des arts du Canada

Greystone Books gratefully acknowledges the xʷməθkʷəy̓əm (Musqueam), Sḵwx̱wú7mesh (Squamish), and səlilwətaɬ (Tsleil-Waututh) peoples on whose land our Vancouver head office is located.

CONTENTS

INTRODUCTION

ON A SUNNY AFTERNOON in June 2005, I stood at my backyard grill with a pair of writer friends as they called me a fool. I was hosting a party for contributors to The Tyee, a journalism website I'd founded a couple of years earlier. The salmon I was barbecuing were a special treat from Alaska's Copper River and I'd paid a pretty penny for them, I told James MacKinnon and Alisa Smith, the couple whose eyebrows shot up before they began to laugh at me.

"What's the deal?" I asked. "Dave," said James, "we have wild salmon just as great right here in British Columbia. And they don't have to arrive by airplane to your plate."

I took their point, if sheepishly, and the conversation continued. Alisa observed that moving food around the world consumed an enormous amount of energy, generating massive global-warming emissions. James added, presciently, fifteen years before a pandemic jammed up the works, that unless we strengthened our local food systems, we were at the mercy of fragile global supply chains.

And that is why, James and Alisa explained, they had been running an experiment by trying to live only on food grown or processed within a hundred miles of their Vancouver apartment.

"You should write about that!" I said. "We are!" they replied. And in unison, it seemed, we named their concept the 100-Mile Diet. The resulting seven-part series published on The Tyee sparked a bestselling book, a television show and a global phenomenon that helped launch the locavore movement.

In that vignette, I think, lie some of the best essences of the British Columbian spirit. A fierce pride of place. A love of this province's natural landscapes and the creatures who inhabit them. A readiness to question what most take for granted. A can-do approach to exploring new paths.

Many people are drawn to this far western side of Canada because spiritually, intellectually, viscerally, they know they belong on that edge. This book offers thirty opportunities to sample such essences, through voices as varied as our sprawling, geographically and culturally diverse province.

Between these pages are some of British Columbia's very best writers. And if you are roaming in search of points of interest, you'd do well to tuck their essays in your bag. Plenty of websites and guidebooks will attend to your tourist needs as you navigate our roads and line up your next good meal. This volume offers something different: emotional resonances to spots on the map.

Think about the best moments you've had while travelling. Did they involve making a serendipitous new friend? Was it the sudden bond formed with a plugged-in local, who leaped to fill you in on some quirky or profound aspect of where you'd just landed? That is what we aimed to recreate with this book.

You have made your way to more than your next stop. You have stumbled into a vibrant soiree. The music is sweet. The mood mixes the funny with the soulful and the wondrous. You are soaking it up as you mention you must be off to your next destination. And someone with a friendly face leans over and says, "Well, if you're going there, have I got a story to tell you!"

ABOUT THE TYEE

ALL OF THE PIECES in this book originally appeared in The Tyee over the past two decades. When The Tyee blinked on in November 2003, it marked the start of an early experiment in independent online journalism. We were a fixture on the internet before Facebook, Twitter, YouTube, smart phones and a lot more digital stuff we now take for granted.

Something else sprang to life at the same moment: a community of writers, artists, innovators and involved readers that has flourished ever since. Today, The Tyee is non-profit and largely reader-funded, an award-winning beacon of hope that public-interest journalism can survive.

In the Indigenous lexicon called Chinook, our name means "leader or authority worthy of respect." Two decades ago, we adopted this name with humility, mindful that the map lines defining this province are a colonial construct, overlaying largely unceded territory belonging to peoples who have lived here since time immemorial.

When Europeans first showed up, First Nations drew from their rich languages to fashion a simpler one—Chinook—for communicating with the newcomers. Other Chinook words you might bump into while travelling around the Salish Sea include *skookum* (strong, brave, impressive), *chuck* (saltwater) and *mucky muck* (plenty of food, one who lives well).

In more recent times, the word *tyee* has also come to mean a feisty, wild salmon weighing over thirty pounds. Which makes it even more laughable, I guess, that I thought I could impress my B.C. pals by serving Alaskan salmon at a Tyee gathering. Ah well. Life is a journey. That moment is now, for me, one more story about the importance of knowing exactly where you are.

DAVID BEERS, founding editor, The Tyee

CRESTON

The Great Arrow Creek Disaster

DOROTHY WOODEND

(2019)

ON A GREY FRIDAY AFTERNOON, I show up at the driving school, housed in a small office at the back of an insurance company, for my first lesson. The instructor, Vincent, cheerfully tells me he has been teaching for thirty years. His students have gone on to become bus drivers and police officers, positions of driving authority. "You'll be fine," he says.

"I haven't driven since 1985. I don't want to kill anyone," I reply. He smiles, albeit with a little less certainty.

After decades of adult life—marriage, a child, work and sundry—one of my biggest shames remains the fact that I never learned to drive.

"Learn to DRIVE." I write it every New Year's, along with "Don't procrastinate, be nicer to people, don't eat chips, go the gym." I've never done any of it.

Now here I am, sitting in the front seat of the car, listening intently to Vincent explain how to stick the key in the ignition and start the engine.

Getting along without a car in the city isn't all that hard. I've been walking, riding a bike or taking the bus since I moved to Vancouver thirty-three years ago. I've made it work. In the meantime, reasons not to get my licence continue to grow. The ethical case against cars is overwhelming. They hurt people. They're

expensive, polluting and wasteful. They run over small animals, knock over mailboxes and are turning the earth into a smelly, hellish furnace.

So, why, after all this time, ruin my spotless non-driving record? What is my real auto motive (heh heh)?

I could offer easy answers. I want to get around better, see new places, feel more independent. But the real reason goes back to a cold night on a lonely highway in the Kootenays when I was sixteen years old. When I tell the nice instructor that I'm afraid I might kill someone, I'm not kidding. What happened that night was a kind of bargain. In the blink of an eye, my own life was spared, but for decades afterwards I've let fear blockade too many turns in the journey.

Not driving has come to stand in for active avoidance instead of facing the things that are fucked up. The crappy part is that fear never really goes away; it just gets parked in a dark garage somewhere, idling in wait.

Some of the details of the night in December 1985 are fuzzy, others sharp as shattered glass.

"Yesterday was the worst day of my life. I'm so glad that I'm here to tell myself about it instead of being in a morgue somewhere. Told Mother who almost pulled out a gun and shot me on sight." I wrote it all down in loopy teenage script in my journal and added a couple of drawings, including a sad, crying face.

I'd had a few tentative driving lessons with my parents, but no one had told me I was ready to take the wheel on my own. We lived in a log house forty kilometres outside of Creston, my twin sister Avril and me, our mother, stepfather, and two younger brothers. Cars were a necessity.

It had already been a tough go in the fall of '85. We didn't have much money. My stepdad, Len, had taken a job up north to make some extra cash. It wasn't as grim as other years, when we'd spent weekends hand-painting wooden toys to sell at the craft market, or hawking Christmas trees in the parking lot of the hardware store at the entrance of town. My brothers were too young and clueless to understand what being poor meant. But my sister and I knew the scalding mortification, praying that no one from school would see you scuffling for a bit of cash, wanting the frozen pavement to crack open and swallow you whole.

Growing up poor is shitty just about anywhere, but in a small town there are particular flavours and nuances. Within the social status system of Creston, the popular girls had beautiful teeth and giant perms. Their brothers played bantam hockey. Their fathers were doctors or businessmen. Their mothers spent a lot of time wandering up and down the aisles of the Overwaitea supermarket. They shaved their legs and their armpits and they always smelled nice in a baby powder kind of way.

It was like they'd been beamed out of a sitcom universe, full of rancher houses and Brady Bunch problems. I was obsessed with them, their rec rooms with padded bar stools, their ready access to Tang and Hostess Twinkies.

My own mother wore a kerchief like a Russian peasant, held women's consciousness-raising meetings in the front room of our tiny trailer, and never met a protest she didn't want to join or lead. Her version of being grown up seemed to consist of drinking endless cups of herbal tea and talking about how depressed you were. The only other models of adulthood on the farm were my grandparents, who had their own issues, mostly around money and non-stop work.

On the farm, children as well as adults were expected to pull their own weight, whether that meant picking cherries in the summer, apples in the fall or rocks in the spring. Picking rocks was like being on a tiny chain gang, walking behind the tractor, hucking chunks of granite from the freshly plowed field onto a cart with all the bad attitude of lifelong convicts.

Before Avril and I turned eleven, we'd already been drafted into operating the tractor by our grandfather, a hard man who'd come of age in the Dirty Thirties. He'd lost his mother to cancer when he was seven and had gone to work when he was twelve. During haying season, he would perch on the hay rake attached to the back of the 1942 Farmall and yell commands in farmer lingo left over from the Great Depression. *Yee* and *haw* meant "Turn right" and "Turn left." *Bigger wheel* meant "Put it in a higher gear." My sister had managed to run him over twice. He'd been fixing the hitch behind the tractor, and when he asked her a question she backed up and pinned him beneath the wheel. When he screamed, she lurched forward and ran over him again. When I was driving the tractor and my grandfather yelled at me for doing something dumb, I tended to freeze at the wheel and try to drive into Kootenay Lake.

Like a lot of what we did on the farm, haying was an insane amount of work. Cutting it was only the beginning. After the stuff had dried, it had to be forked by hand onto an ancient contraption that my grandfather had welded together out of old bedframes. We used it as an impromptu jungle gym the rest of the year. We kids had developed some strategies to get out of work and do the stuff we really wanted to do, like watching TV in the daytime or jumping in the hayloft. A scout, usually one of my brothers, would watch for my grandfather's tall figure stalking across the pasture. When someone hissed "Grandpa's coming!" we'd scramble in panic. But sometimes he caught us unawares. I remember having a child-sized heart attack when the door to the trailer slammed open one day and he came barrelling in to catch us watching *Gilligan's Island* on a sunny afternoon. "Don't work, don't eat!" he yelled and stomped off, mad at the weather, mad at the cherry trees and especially mad at lazy goddamn kids.

By the time we were teenagers, the urge to escape was like a brush fire. There was only one road out of town. To use it, you needed to know how to drive. From across the province, the city of Vancouver beckoned at night, when its radio signal came in clear, promising a world full of nightclubs, cool clothes, glamour and wide-open possibility.

THAT DECEMBER OF 1985, Len was away, but a guy named Mike, a twenty-something grifter who'd been kicked out by his parents, had battened onto us like a big, blond tick. He'd helped Len put the roof on our log house and then simply never left. At the time, he was sleeping on our living room floor and eating all our food, because no one quite knew how to get rid of him. Naturally, I was madly in love with him.

I don't know why my mother let Mike and me have the car that particular night in December. Maybe she wasn't paying attention. Probably we were being annoying, hanging around, being bored. Whatever the reason, my mother gave me the key, attached to her hand-tooled leather keychain embossed with the words "Free Female." Off we went. "You know how to drive, right?" Mike asked. Instead of saying "Not really," I said "Sure!" and hopped in behind the wheel. For a while, things went okay. It was dark and very cold, but the roads were dry, and for a moment I thought, "Hey, I'm actually doing this!" That's the moment when fate raised its middle finger.

We'd been circling about the back roads for a while and were getting ready to turn around and go back when it happened. We hit a patch of black ice, and instead of jamming my foot on the brake, I stomped the gas pedal to the floor and the car took off like a rocket. We flew.

There were tracks in the snow where we went off the highway, and then a long blank space where the car was airborne for a few seconds. The first power pole exploded on contact. It was old and rotten and the top half of it bounced off the roof of the car, leaving a perfectly round indentation. The second pole snapped in half and the third simply fell over sideways like a drunk passing out against a wall.

The car came to rest at the bottom of a snowbank. The first thing I remember is the high-pitched whine of the still-running engine. Mike reached over and lifted my leg off the gas pedal. "Stay in the car," he said, nodding at the downed power lines writhing and sparking outside on the highway. The front of the car was caved in, looking like a V for Victory. Steam emerged from it like a kettle on hard boil.

At that point, things went blank. I don't really remember the RCMP arriving and taking us back home. I next recall I was laughing, the nervous panicky kind, when I told my mother, "I wrecked the car." I watched the smile slowly slide off her face when she realized I wasn't kidding. Then the yelling started. My brother Geronimo, hiding behind her legs, said, "Thanks for wrecking Christmas, Dorothy." I made a mental note to beat the living hell out of him.

I do remember one of the officers, before they stepped back into the night, saying to my mother, "Don't let this one drive."

The accident knocked out the power to a good portion of West Creston, and to this day it is referred to in family history as the Great Arrow Creek Disaster. No one died, except for the poor car and three power poles. That I'd survived, I misspelled in my diary, was "pretty dam miraculous." But afterwards, no one would teach me how to drive.

My twin, Avril, learned to drive later that same year, which began a social experiment that has shaped our relationship and our roles ever since. She would be the one entrusted to steer, to navigate risk and safely get us from point A to point B. I would be the dumb passenger, rendered dependent by my inferred incompetence, suitable only for switching cassette tapes and offering onboard entertainment. At driving, that most basic life skill (and therefore how many others?), I was deemed a menace to myself and those around me.

The other day Avril, who is the most capable and competent human I know, observed, "You're a different person when you drive."

I've decided I've had enough after a lifetime of letting chickenshit stuff take the wheel. Enough, after all the decisions made or unmade because of that one night when I was too eager to grow up and get moving. That one night when I asked my mother for the keys, and I left so much crumpled and smoking by the side of the road.

Dear reader, consider yourself warned. I am determined to learn how to drive.

QUICK FACTS ABOUT CRESTON

- Creston has never observed daylight saving time.
- The Ktunaxa Nation, in whose territory Creston is located, calls the area Yaqan Nukiy, meaning "where the rock stands."
- The Creston Valley—and its rich, fertile soil, which makes it perfect for agriculture—was created twelve thousand years ago by melting glaciers.

KRESTOVA

Newcomers to Doukhobor Territory

LEESA DEAN

(2023)

THE FIRST TIME I went to Krestova, I'd been living in West Kootenay for a year when the man I would one day marry invited me to join him for nachos where he was house-sitting. He drew a map in symbols that led me past Frog Peak Café, over the Slocan River and up a long and winding hill, past the "Keep Krestova Wild" sign, past the horse stables, past Linden Lane Farms, to the plateau of land known as Krestova. That night, we took a long walk on Cemetery Road. It was September. The coming shift in season was palpable; the bright red of late tomatoes still glistened in vast gardens.

Fast-forward six years and my husband, daughter and I now live on Pass Creek Road, at the bottom of what's called Pump Hill, a steep and treacherous road that used to be a water corridor between the plateau and where we live. Some call our area Lower Krestova, others Crescent Valley, and some of the old-timers still call it Goose Creek. We call it home.

We moved here in 2017, shortly before the birth of our daughter, having stumbled upon a For Sale sign during the Columbia Basin Culture Tour—a weekend when artists in towns and settlements along the Columbia River open their homes and studios to the public. We weren't looking for a house in the country, but the area

drew us in. The land itself had good sun exposure, and I loved the wildness evoked by the landscape. A creek borders the property, and I feel most alive when I'm near fast-running water.

Since Krestova is unincorporated, meaning it has no local municipal government, the actual territory it covers is subjective. But everyone agrees that the "plateau" is Krestova. This is where the Doukhobors, a mostly pacifist, anti-materialist Christian sect who fled Russian persecution, originally settled in 1929. They arrived during a mass migration in 1899 and eventually made their way to areas of West Kootenay, including Krestova, where they lived communal, non-materialistic lifestyles. Author Vera Maloff illuminates this local history in her 2020 memoir *Our Backs Warmed by the Sun: Memories of a Doukhobor Life*, and Robert Chursinoff's recently released novel, *The Descendants*, explores it through a fictional lens.

Despite these pacifist underpinnings, if you were to travel down Cemetery Road about seventy years ago, in the late 1950s and early 1960s, you might have witnessed homes engulfed in flames. Those were the homes of Doukhobor Freedomites, also referred to as Sons of Freedom, a subset of radical Doukhobors led by Stefan Sorokin who were involved in anti-government bombings, most notably the 1962 tower bombing—a 366-foot structure built by West Kootenay Power was destroyed, cutting off the electric supply to several communities on the other side of Kootenay Lake.

Some of the burning homes in Krestova belonged to families whose children were taken from them during "Operation Snatch" and sent to a prison-like school in New Denver, B.C., where they faced conditions similar to the residential schools where Indigenous children were sent. The homes were set on fire by their owners, in an attempt to demonstrate their freedom from material possessions.

In 1962, a group of them marched over five hundred kilometres west, to Agassiz, B.C., where many of their family members had been imprisoned as a result of the conflicts and bombings.

Natasha Makortoff is our neighbour on the other side of the creek. She and her husband, Andy, both lived in the Agassiz prison camp as children. Although she doesn't remember much from her time there—she left as a young child—she fondly remembers being one of the first three families to move to the New Settlement, a community just up the road from us that was established specifically for some of the families who had been imprisoned in Agassiz.

"For the first year, we didn't have running water," she tells me. There was no electricity in the community until around 1988, though some families had generators.

Most of the original homes in Krestova were built without foundations, and without siding. Even today, some of the houses remain unfinished, but the change in demographic is also noticeable. Many of the original Doukhobor families have passed or moved on, and some of the newer, more modern houses seem to counter the very spirit of Doukhobor simplicity with their expansive floor plans and manicured lawns.

What Natasha remembers most about growing up in the New Settlement is the sense of community and the excitement of roaming free with so many other children who experienced similar upbringings. I walk there often with my daughter, especially in summer, when we can explore the trails and swimming holes along Goose Creek. The roads up there are still unpaved, and there's no through traffic. In late August, there is usually a stand of free zucchinis near the large sign at the entrance, which outlines the history of the New Settlement. Parts of the sign have faded over the years, but the message is still clear: it was a community built on hope.

We met our other neighbours slowly. At first, we were known as the young couple who often walked to the nearby waterfall. Our daughter grew, toddled along beside us and learned to ride a bike while passing cars offered a wide berth. In winter, reaching for snowflakes in her bright red coat, she stood out. We were otherwise innocuous, a few more new faces in an evolving rural landscape.

But eventually that changed. My husband, a mural artist, grew tired of sneaking around trainyards late at night in search of paintable surfaces and decided to create his own outdoor gallery.

In the spring of 2020, he erected a large billboard on the edge of our property, facing the highway, to be used as a canvas for experimentation and political expression. The billboard went up shortly before George Floyd was murdered, and his first piece was a Black Lives Matter tribute. He stood in the early spring sun, spray can poised, and people slowed down, curious to see what would materialize from his initial sketch lines. Eventually, it became a dystopian scene of police brutality, with the initials "BLM," for "Black Lives Matter," large and bold at the centre.

Now the neighbours knew who we were.

Our understanding of the neighbourhood has evolved largely based on responses to this public art. Most of the responses are positive—one of the first neighbours to stop and introduce herself was a young Black woman from the plateau who thanked my husband for the mural and told him it made her feel safe and seen.

Later that week, though, a long-time Doukhobor resident of the area informed us that he thought the BLM movement was racist. He said we didn't have the right to do any of the things we were doing—the land belonged to the department of highways. We countered that we are all on Indigenous land, but besides that, the billboard was on our property line, and more importantly, BLM is an anti-racist movement. We told him we were both educators at a nearby college; he said we should be fired.

The Krestova community Facebook group provides another window into the ways in which our area is both highly factionary and deeply community-minded. The discussion board is where you can expect degenerative conversations on a variety of topics, ranging from violent threats against children on dirt bikes and the spandex-clad cyclists on Pass Creek Road to inordinate levels of rage against proposed noise bylaws—some people really want to keep Krestova "wild," even if it means normalizing random gunfire, a recent hot topic. On a regular basis, a community member will tell someone who displays interest in things like organized governance to "go back to the *#&-ing city."

At the same time, the Facebook group is also where we organize events like the annual slow food drive, where residents cycle from house to house, visiting and purchasing home-cooked meals, produce and locally made crafts. For Halloween, data is collected to create a trick-or-treating map, since the distances between houses can be difficult to navigate. And this fall, we were able to rally support for Krestova Regional Park. Together, we raised $475,000 in less than two months to purchase community lands that had been put up for private sale—though the park wasn't established without friction. The land itself was put up for sale because of conflict among the Doukhobor families who owned the titles, and some fear that the park, having been funded mostly by non-Doukhobor donors, will lose sight of the area's historical roots.

Ironically, it often feels like, in a community this small, we have to hold larger spaces for each other. The man who told us we should be fired from the college also delivered us three cords of wood right before the cold season settled in, treating us with respect when he did so. Another person, who has told me to go back to the city at least twice, offered to jump my car when the battery died.

And as my husband's art billboards have multiplied in number over the years, the number of friends we have in the community has also multiplied, in part as a result of his art. Community members bring him gifts—beer, magic mushrooms, cookies and cash donations for paint. He fills the billboards with vintage cartoons that bond the community through nostalgia, portraits of our daughter, and, more recently, pleas for peace in Ukraine. This fall, he painted an "Every Child Matters" mural in support of Indigenous children and youth. An Indigenous resident of the plateau smudged the wall and expressed her deep gratitude.

While my husband was painting the mural, a neighbour struck up a conversation with him, reminding him about Operation Snatch. "You know," she said, "our children were taken, too."

Living here, we are constantly prompted to remember the complexities of all the histories and social layers woven into this wild and beautiful landscape.

QUICK FACTS ABOUT KRESTOVA

→ Krestova was first settled in 1908 by Doukhobor pioneers who immigrated from Ukraine and Russia in 1899, assisted by novelist Leo Tolstoy, British and American Quakers and Russian anarchists.

→ Doukhobors initially arrived in Saskatchewan; however, when the Canadian government reneged on its promise of communally owned land, the group's leader, Peter "Lordly" Verigin, led a group of around 7,500 west to British Columbia—one of the largest organized internal migrations in Canadian history.

→ The name Krestova comes from the Russian *Dolina Krestova*, which means "valley of the cross."

OKANAGAN INDIAN BAND RESERVE

"Everything Is Burning and Your House Is Gone"

MICHELLE GAMAGE

(2021)

THE BURNT-BLACK FOREST IS SILENT. A wind blows through, pushing chilly October fingers around the charred remains of trees. But it doesn't make a sound—there are no leaves to rustle on the trees, no small branches to sway, no bushes on the ground.

The snap as my co-worker sets up his tripod makes me jump. I can see him about a hundred metres away and up a hill. He's positioning his camera to try and capture the devastation. I'm holding a recorder, similarly wanting to capture the eeriness of the forest. But there's nothing to record except the strange crunch my hiking boots make as I walk across the chalky forest floor.

Everything smells like a soggy campfire. The sky is grey. Farther down the mountain there's a scattering of bright-orange pine trees. The fire's heat cooked their needles, but the flames didn't reach their trunks. I've been seeing this same strange orange on the periphery of all the burns, on deciduous and evergreen trees alike. I'm told that means they're likely dead and will have to be cut down.

This is the aftermath of the White Rock Lake fire. The BC Wildfire Service says the fire was discovered July 13, 2021, cause unknown, and was still smouldering in

parts of the province as the first snow started to fall in late October. It devoured over a hundred homes as it ripped through the Okanagan Indian Band Reserve, Killiney Beach, Estamont—communities on the northwest shore of Okanagan Lake, about forty minutes north of Kelowna—and Monte Lake, another forty-minute drive to the west, along the highway toward Kamloops.

The White Rock Lake fire was the third biggest of 1,630 fires in B.C. that year, when wildfires displaced nearly 33,000 people and killed two.

The White Rock Lake fire burned 83,342 hectares, an area seven times the size of Vancouver, and caused at least $77 million in insured damage. But the true cost is much higher—a lot of people in remote, off-grid or Indigenous communities can't access insurance.

Insurance companies are often hesitant or unwilling to insure buildings in remote or Indigenous communities, says Jason Thistlethwaite, an associate professor at the School of Environment, Enterprise and Development at the University of Waterloo.

They're conservative businesses that don't want to offer coverage when they think they'll have to eventually pay out, he says. So companies will refuse to insure homes built far away from emergency services or infrastructure, or in areas more prone to environmental disasters like flooding or wildfires. That includes many Indigenous communities because of the legacy of colonialism, Thistlethwaite says.

During ten days in the Interior, I meet six people who didn't have insurance and lost their homes.

In the forest, the fire charred trees and ate down into the forest floor, where it burned stumps, leaving strange holes with octopus-like arms stretching off in different directions. When it found communities, it devoured entire neighbourhoods.

"IT WAS REALLY HARD that night," says Tiffany Wilson, who is from the Syilx Nation, a member of the Okanagan Indian Band and a mother of three. She lost her home in the fire.

"Everyone was listening to the BC Wildfire radio," she says. "Knowing the firefighters were in this area, hearing them say 'There's cars back here, we need to get out.' That meant it was in one of two places, either my kid's dad's backyard, or ours. And it was here."

Tiffany's dark hair is pulled back in a ponytail and she's wearing a puffy eggplant-coloured vest with a tiny orange T-shirt pinned over her heart. She's standing next to the shell of what once was her home. She stoops and picks up a blackened silver picture frame. The image is charred and blistered, but family members are still recognizable, decked out in 1980s-era glasses and grinning at the camera. She brushes off some ash, then quietly sighs and gently places the picture back on the ground.

Four generations of her family lived in the home, and it would have soon been five—Wilson's oldest daughter is pregnant.

Tiffany's extended family had built their homes within walking distance of one another on a lush, sprawling property originally cleared by her grandfather and his mother. When the fire came through, it destroyed several family homes—her aunt's next door, her cousins', and her uncle's just up the road.

Her eighty-one-year-old grandfather, William Wilson, has lived on the property for seventy-five years. His bushy white moustache is neatly combed and his deeply lined face is pulled down in a scowl, though his voice is soft and thoughtful when he speaks. He wears a white cowboy hat and a heavy black-denim aviator coat. Like Tiffany, William is a member of the Okanagan Indian Band and Syilx Nation. They speak the nsyilxcən language, part of the Salish language family.

William, who lived under the same roof as Tiffany, is a farmer who mainly grows hay for feed. He has often kept horses and cattle, though he'd sold his cows a couple years before the fire.

"I've seen fires like this before, but never this close. And there's never been any homes burnt before from the fires," he says. "This fire season was worse. There was a long dry period in the spring with no rain. Last time we had something like that was '63 or '65. The ground was just tinder dry."

On the Okanagan Indian Band Reserve, the White Rock Lake fire damaged twelve homes and destroyed another ten. It also took out Little Kingdom, a convenience store and community hub that sold fresh baked goods, groceries, clothes, tools, gardening accessories, gas and cannabis, all under one roof.

William took some clothes with him when he evacuated, but left everything else he owned behind. He lost family photos, his boats and a motorhome. He lost saddles, gear, skates and clothes. He lost his tractors and his generator. His horses, grazing in the field next to us as we talk, thankfully survived.

The next day, we drive a half-hour from a hotel in Vernon back to the family property with Tiffany's uncle, Henry Wilson, who is also a member of the Okanagan Indian Band and Syilx Nation. Henry has agreed to come with us to see his house—the first time he's been back since the fire. As we drive toward his home, we play the Doors. His eyes crinkle a little—they're his favourite. Henry's Doors collection, which he took with him during the evacuation, is now one of the few belongings he has left.

As we get closer to the property, the morning's fog suddenly gives way to sunlight. Fall colours of brilliant yellows and reds blush across the rolling landscape, covered in trees here and grassland there. Farm stands dot the roadside, offering heaping bags of crisp apples, zingy salad mixes and sugary late-season grapes. Even the cows grazing in the wide-open fields have a view of the glittering Okanagan Lake.

A black dog with salt-and-pepper patches comes to meet us as we pull into Henry's driveway. Henry steps out and calls to her, but his shoulder-length hair is pulled back by a thick headband and he's wearing a blue medical mask. She gives a nervous bark.

"Daisy, it's me, you goofball," he says, pulling his mask down.

Daisy, who hasn't seen Henry since the fire, attempts to jump up and lick his face, run figure eights between his legs, and bury her face in his hands all at once.

"What do you think, Daisy? What did they do to our house?" he asks her softly, running his hand over her silky coat. "I know, I know. They took our house."

He stands silently for several minutes, staring at the pile of stucco and twisted metal that used to be his home. Daisy leans against him, wagging her tail rhythmically, and he rests his hand on her head.

Henry says he is angry because he was told if he stayed to fight the fire, no firefighters would come to his property to help, and because he was told sprinklers would be set up around his house—but the sprinklers never arrived. Now his house is rubble.

Tiffany says when Okanagan Indian Band members tried to protect their property, the RCMP told them they could leave on their own or in the back of a police car.

An officer in charge of the Vernon North Okanagan RCMP told The Tyee officers were not given orders to forcibly remove people. "There was no hard line regarding persons leaving zones," they wrote in an email.

RCMP officers would have told Okanagan Indian Band members about the evacuation order and advised them that first responders would not be able to come back for them if the "situation deteriorated," the officer said. But "under no circumstances were persons removed—if there was someone who said they had no way out, they could have been told that the RCMP officer could take them."

Next door to Henry lives his nephew, Dan Wilson, a member of the Okanagan Indian Band and Syilx Nation whose house was mostly spared by the fire, save one corner where the heat blistered the paint. Daisy the dog lives with him.

Indigenous Services Canada will help fund the rebuilding of the houses that were burned on the reserve, says Dan, past Chief of the Okanagan Indian Band and councillor, who spoke to The Tyee as a private citizen affected by the fire rather than in an official capacity.

The Wilsons are worried the process won't be smooth.

"People from [Indigenous Services Canada] don't realize a lot of these homes housed more than one family," Tiffany says. "We had four generations living in our house, soon to be five. We're only getting two temporary homes here."

Henry was told he'd be in temporary housing back on his property in the late fall. He's hoping they won't need to turn to the courts to make the federal government follow through on its commitments.

"Climate change is caused by industry. They should be paying more to clean everything up—they did it all," Henry says as he looks at the heap that once was his sturdy home.

"They make corporations, then they hide behind them. Can't touch a corporation with the law," he adds.

"I think the laws of nature should come before everything."

THIRTEEN KILOMETRES down the road from the Wilsons, heading north toward Vernon, Sandra Eberle runs On the Way, a food truck with a cheerfully decorated patio and an outdoor pizza oven.

In between cooking, taking orders and chatting up everyone who stops to order her food, Sandra introduces us to her husband, Charles Eberle, and to Russell Cadotte, a Saulteaux Lakota man who has called the Okanagan home his entire life.

Eberle and Cadotte help fire crews during the summer by building the expansive water infrastructure needed to fight a wildfire. They're avid amateur photographers and their stories from the summer are punctuated with pictures on their phones—blood-red midday skies; dozens of fire trucks screaming down smoky highways; pumping stations set up on the side of sparkling lakes. A video captures the size of the wall of smoke that came off the White Rock Lake fire—it takes up half the sky.

Eberle describes the process of using pumping stations to send the water necessary to fight the fires up steep hills before it can be used to fill fire trucks or other containers. Then there's the task of setting up sprinklers to protect homes. It's a logistical nightmare with huge amounts of coordination required—it'd be bad to burst a hose when the flames are headed your way.

"The government really needs to respect local knowledge when fighting fires," Cadotte says. "There's people who spend almost their entire lives in the bush around here—hunters, you know. They know what trees grow where, what the land is like, where the water is. The government should work with them out in the backwoods, but doesn't."

Everyone we speak with praises the efforts of the crews on the ground fighting the fires—emphasizing their bravery and worrying about the trauma fire crews experience while facing down infernos that are consuming their hometowns, or even their own homes.

But when management doesn't involve locals, it can slow down firefighting efforts in remote areas, and Cadotte say.

The BC Wildfire Service hires crews for its six fire centres across B.C. every spring, mainly from the local areas so that fire crews "are familiar with their local fire centre's terrain, tree types and fire behaviour," says Briana Hill, the service's fire information officer, in an email. The service also hires local equipment operators and local liaison officers, and works closely with local Indigenous fire crews, Hill says.

Hill adds that during the White Rock Lake fire, local industry and equipment operators were used to help build roads so fire crews could do "wildfire suppression."

For her part, Sandra Eberle is critical of both insurance companies and the inadequate housing on the reserve.

"We don't have proper homes for Natives out here. These houses don't have a proper furnace, drinkable water—nothing! It's bullshit," she says.

"People have to rough it out here in the winter, and now with the heat in the summer too because houses don't have any insulation. And the water? Hah! You wouldn't even feed it to your dog. There's no gas either."

Insurance companies, she says, often decline to insure the homes because of the condition they're in.

Rob Bouchard, whose home was off-grid in Monte Lake, wasn't able to get insurance either. His eighty-acre property is off a steep, winding, rough road that goes several kilometres up a hillside.

The White Rock Lake fire destroyed his home, two buildings, a car park and every tree on his property. Now all that's left is a burned cement foundation, heaped high with a chalky pile of ash and stone. He clambers to the top of it and gestures to the surrounding 360-degree view of the sprawling landscape.

The trees that ringed the home, shielding the property from the wind, are gone. The land tumbles steeply into the wide valley of Monte Lake. The view is of farmland down below, and fire-charred hillside. Bouchard wasn't able to find an insurance company that would sell him insurance for his home, which he moved into six years ago.

"I said, 'All right, I guess we're on our own'—not expecting a crazy wildfire like this to come through," he says, pulling his black baseball cap down over close-cropped ginger hair as October rain starts to fall.

There are a lot of reasons companies refuse to insure a home, the University of Waterloo's Thistlethwaite says—everything from credit rating to the quality of the house and how likely it is the house will be damaged in the future, as well as how likely it is that a homeowner will continue paying for insurance and ownership. This can complicate insurance for some Indigenous communities, where property isn't owned individually but by band councils, he adds. And it's complicated for homeowners like Bouchard, whose home is a fairly remote cabin conversion completed without permits.

Climate change is also changing who can access insurance.

"A major risk of climate change is that insurance becomes a luxury for the rich," Thistlethwaite says. That's bad news for remote and Indigenous communities, which are generally poorer and more exposed to climate change than large cities.

To prevent that from happening, Canada could explore alternative insurance models, like public, group or parametric insurance, which pays out when a predefined event happens, rather than when damage occurs. Another possibility is public insurance that could cover remote areas for claims higher than, say, $20,000 in damages, Thistlethwaite says. Private insurance companies might be more willing to cover remote areas if they know they'd only be on the hook for $20,000.

Bouchard remained for as long as he could on the night of the fire, staying behind to do everything he could think of to protect his home after his wife, kids and pets had left. Then the fire, from over the ridge, spat out a massive plume of smoke, and "everyone I know started phoning or texting me saying, 'You gotta get out of there. Leave. Now.'"

Once he was safely in the valley below, he turned to see the wildfire appear. It looked like a wall of flames, Bouchard says, at least three kilometres long. He watched images on his phone from his home security camera that showed the fire rush past his house. Then sparks appeared inside. Then the feed cut out.

Bouchard says he was never contacted directly by anyone in government—no firefighters, no search-and-rescue workers—before or after the fire. The only reason his family knew to evacuate was because they saw a blue ribbon tied to the gate at the end of their driveway. They had to look up what it meant.

The day after the fire, he and some neighbours illegally returned to the area to fight small fires still smouldering in the community.

A spokesperson for the Thompson-Nicola Regional District said the White Rock Lake fire destroyed thirty-two primary dwellings in the region, with most of the damage happening in Monte Lake. The remote community has about 120 addresses, but not all of those are homes, the spokesperson noted.

Bouchard estimates that without community efforts, thirty to fifty percent more homes would have burned.

People in Monte Lake are angry with the government. Near the community's post office/liquor store sits a shipping container with "GOVT. ARSON" spray-painted on the side in letters as tall as a person. Outside the post office a notice is tacked to the community flyer board calling on residents to join a class-action lawsuit against the government.

The BC Wildfire Service's Hill says forty local residents were paid for their firefighting work in Monte Lake.

"The White Rock Lake wildfire was an incredibly dynamic incident, impacting multiple communities," Hill said in an email to The Tyee. "When it is safe and possible to do so, the BC Wildfire Service strives to support local responses to wildfire suppression. However, due to the emergency nature of wildfire events, decisions are sometimes made before relevant contractual agreements can be completed."

Bouchard spent the summer unsuccessfully trying to find a contractor, and on this day an icy rain is falling, soon to be snow. The whole family wants to be able to stay on their property again as soon as they can, so he's going to build their home himself.

IN KILLINEY BEACH, a small community on the shores of Okanagan Lake, twenty minutes south of the Okanagan Indian Band Reserve, we join Alex Van Bruksvoort, the on-call fire chief for North Westside Fire Rescue.

Killiney Beach is part of the Regional District of Central Okanagan, where roughly 3,000 people were evacuated from 1,316 homes threatened by the White Rock Lake fire between mid-August and early September. The fire destroyed seventy-five homes in the area.

Given the season's wildfire conditions, it's a miracle that no firefighters were killed, Van Bruksvoort says.

He worked alongside fire crews from every corner of B.C. this summer, and had a hundred fire trucks deployed. He tells us about how strong the wind was the night most of the surrounding community burned, and about the impossibility of fighting such an intense wildfire.

When the fire is that hot, all that's left to do is to get out of the way and wait for it to burn itself down, he says. Only then is it safe to come in behind it and help douse whatever is on fire.

Sometimes, when a house is in the path of a fire and there's nothing they can do to stop it, he'll give two firefighters five minutes to run into a house, strip the pillowcases off a bed and cram whatever seems important into those pillowcases, like bedside pictures, he says. The pillowcases get thrown into the back of a truck as they evacuate the area, pulling crews out as the house burns.

Even when death is not part of the equation, post-traumatic stress disorder is still a risk for fire crews, Van Bruksvoort adds. Over his twenty-seven-year career, he's known three firefighters who died by suicide because of lasting trauma.

But there's hope—the culture around mental health is changing in the industry, Van Bruksvoort says. He's even had one person reach out to talk about their trauma from this summer. That's a big step, he says.

While we're at the fire hall, Van Bruksvoort's team runs drills, gearing up and piling into the fire truck as its lights flash. The cool weather of fall is here, but next year's fire season is always just around the corner.

The scars from this season's fires are visible even here at the fire hall. Van Bruksvoort points to some trees metres away from the building that are burned black.

When asked if he's worried for next year's fire season, he shrugs. Maybe next year will be worse, sure, but maybe it'll be like the last two summers, which have had more rain and less fire, he says.

This is a point of view shared by most of the people we meet in the Interior. There doesn't seem to be a looming sense of climate doom—a certainty that each season will be worse than the last.

Every single person we speak with says they can see how the weather is getting hotter and dryer, how the winter season is getting shorter. But when we ask directly if the wildfires are caused by climate change, people shrug, shake their heads, cross their arms. Only one person outright denies that climate change is happening—but many others seem uncomfortable with acknowledging the idea that climate change played into destroying their home and community.

FIVE MINUTES down the road from Killiney Beach on the west side of Okanagan Lake, Camille Steele and her son Thorin Leighty lived with the rest of their family in Estamont before the fire consumed their three-storey home.

It's a jumbled heap now, with chunks of charred trees toppled on top of the rubble. Steele finds a piece of the granite counter from her kitchen, and shows me how you can crumble it with your hands after the fire has cooked it.

Steele's home, tucked in a quiet neighbourhood with rolling lawns, used to have a 180-degree view of the lake. She had a nectarine tree that overflowed with fruit, which she shared with her neighbours every summer.

"We had HardiePlank siding and a metal roof—all the things you're supposed to have to fireproof your house. Obviously, it's no match for Mother Nature," she says, gesturing to the solid steel frame of an exercise machine. The steel bar is bent, warped by the heat of the fire.

Steele learned her house was gone at 4 a.m. on August 17, 2021, her daughter's thirteenth birthday.

But the family had insurance, and is working to catalogue what they've lost, clear the foundation and rebuild.

"As terrible as it is right now, one day it's going to be a memory in the past and it's just going be more like a big life event, instead of something as traumatic as it seems now, you know?" she says. She gives a small smile, shrugs and turns back to poking at the ashes with her sneakers. There's supposed to be a fireproof box somewhere in the rubble, but it hasn't turned up yet.

Steele's quiet neighbourhood was destroyed by the fire, which burned through around seventy-five homes along the residential stretch of the lake.

What wildfire consumes entirely and what it leaves untouched can sometimes seem bizarre. Down by the lakeside in Steele's neighbourhood, one house stands, paint unblistered, green plants in the garden. Next door, barely six metres away, a house burned so hot that all that remains are twisted pieces of metal, warped glass bottles, a two-storey fireplace jutting above the ruin and the chalky remains of drywall. The garden wall shows the ghostly charcoal shadow of what once was a trellis. The next house down the road is untouched.

Bill Drinkwater's home, which was a short walk from Steele's, was also destroyed in the fire. He and his wife, Elaine Drinkwater, are staying at a neighbour's summer cottage, which was left standing.

Bill shows us what remains of his home: a water tank, a tool box, a heap of mugs piled in the ash and a pair of old metal piggy banks that belonged to his children. The coins inside have all melted together.

The garden surrounding the house was once an Eden of tumbling bramble roses full of blooms, Elaine Drinkwater says. She uses a cane for support as we wander around her blackened garden with cracked teal and blue ceramic pots. She explains how quail would roost in the roses, and deer would wander through as she sat, drinking tea or absorbed in a book. In the spring the garden was a riot of purples as butterfly bushes blossomed and the magnolia tree blushed pink. Small birds would land on her shoulder and cheekily demand food.

The Drinkwaters heard they'd lost their home from a neighbour who'd tried to stay and fight the fire. "He texted around midnight, saying, 'I can't stay any longer, everything is burning and your house is gone,'" Bill says. "It's been hard. When you're in your seventies, you don't want to be having to start from a suitcase again."

Elaine and Bill first returned to see the house around Labour Day. Neighbours gathered in their driveway, half who'd lost their homes and half who hadn't. "They were crying, and crying for me," she says. "And I said, 'I can't cry. If I cry I'm not going to be able to carry on.'"

Elaine is one of the few people we meet who names climate change as a cause of the fires.

"It was hotter," she says of the climate change–worsened fire. "It burned more intensely."

I stand with the Drinkwaters and watch a herd of deer pick their way down the burned hillside. A flock of quail startle and come scuttling out of the remains of one of Elaine's bramble rose bushes. There's life here, and more and more bits of green are starting to poke their way out of the blackened soil.

But it'll take generations for the trees and animal populations to recover, Elaine says. Longer than she expects to be alive. And, she notes, a certain amount of climate change is baked in and B.C. has many more unprecedented, record-breaking fire seasons coming.

"I feel what we've done here is profoundly wrong," she says, talking again about climate change. "I'm not happy with the world we've left."

QUICK FACTS ABOUT THE OKANAGAN INDIAN BAND RESERVE

- The Okanagan Indian Band comprises seven bands, and the combined total of their lands is 11,282 hectares.
- The people of the Okanagan Indian Band are part of the Syilx Nation. *Sqílxʷ* is the nsyilxcən word for "Indigenous person," and translates to "the dream in a spiral."
- In the 1860s, thousands of mounted Syilx Okanagan warriors gathered at the head of Okanagan Lake, threatening war should the Crown take Syilx Okanagan land rights. The Crown acquiesced and formally set aside territory for the Syilx Okanagan Nation.

OSOYOOS DESERT

To Honour the Lost, a Cattle Drive

KATE HELMORE

(2022)

RAIN FALLS ON THE SAND DUNES as five horse riders set out across the Osoyoos desert.

The riders are hunched in their saddles, the rain dripping off the brims of their stetson hats and soaking the flanks of their horses. The riders and horses are black silhouettes against a landscape dyed grey by fog.

This weather is unusual. Last year, temperatures in B.C.'s Interior hit forty-five degrees in June. Charred tree stumps and the skeletons of animals still litter the ground—testament to the forest fires that followed. But this year the land is lush and green. Perfect forage for wandering cows.

"Rattlesnake," says Elijah Swan-Hall, who, at fifteen, is the youngest. He peers into the bush and listens for the *tsk tsk tsk*. His grandfather was bitten by one a few years ago, he says. He survived, but the finger on his right hand is still crooked at the joint. "He's a tough guy," Swan-Hall says, lighting a cigarette.

The Stelkia family cattle drive always begins this way. On the first day, riders search the desert for cows scattered across the Osoyoos Indian Reserve, which abuts the U.S. border an hour and a half south of Kelowna.

On the second day, the cows will be corralled together

at Spetlumkum ranch, owned by the Stelkia family, who are Syilx—but who prefer to be referred to as Indian.

"It is part of our heritage," Aaron Stelkia, the chief cattle rancher of the Stelkia family, told me a few months ago, while I was interviewing him for another story. "We don't want that word to be forgotten."

On the third day, the cattle will be pushed around twelve kilometres southwest up the mountain, where lush, green grass will sustain them over the summer and fall, until the frost and snow force them back down into the valley in the winter.

The riders pass by a graveyard. The Osoyoos Indian Band flag flutters in the wind above rows of tombstones. Swan-Hall knows many of the people in this cemetery. Aunts, uncles and cousins.

A stone's throw across the road from the cemetery are the charred remains of a church burned down a year ago, barely a month after 215 unmarked graves were found at the site of the Kamloops Indian Residential School.

The cattle drive is not just a practical necessity for the Stelkias. It is also a pilgrimage across residential school land done in memory of all the children lost. In particular, for Shaun Stelkia, who drowned in Wood Lake, a two-hour drive north of here. He died eight years ago at the age of twenty-nine.

But in the middle of the desert, mounted on a horse, the riders feel like Shaun's still around. "The drive means family," Swan-Hall says. "We may no longer be physically connected to each other. But out there, on the land, we're spiritually and mentally connected."

After four hours of riding, the riders find the cows in a steep ravine, hidden alongside a creek and knee-deep in mud. They number around sixty, calves included. They must now be pushed up the hill and onto the flats, where they will be corralled in a pasture, ready for day two.

THE RAIN HAS STOPPED and the clouds start to dissipate as the second day of the cattle drive begins. As the sun emerges from behind the rolling hills that encircle the Osoyoos desert, the fog lifts, the soft ground hardens and the air turns amber and gold, a perfect complement to the wiry, yellow grass that—alongside silvery, thigh-high sagebrush—covers the earth.

Riders sink back into their saddles, the soft flesh of their thighs rubbed raw from hours of riding yesterday.

Today, the cows must be pushed five kilometres to another ranch where the remainder wait, ready to be charged into the mountains.

It won't be a quick five kilometres. The cows are slow, and sometimes ornery. Some riders will push from the back, while others will cover the flanks, their presence forcing the cows to stay in line.

"Pushing cows is like playing pool," says Jessi Wyatt, who was galloping racehorses at five years old. "You're the cue ball and you've gotta apply just the right amount of pressure at just the right angle if you wanna get it to go the right place."

Wyatt grew up on a ranch. She spent fifteen years working at feedlots, feeding cattle and racing horses between stalls. But these days she takes tourists on trail rides, where she teaches inexperienced riders to stay in the saddle. And she also trains wild horses.

"Like my grandfather said, the key to staying in the saddle is simple," she jokes. "Shoulders like a lady, hips like a... belly dancer."

Wyatt does the job Shaun Stelkia used to do. And her son is named after him.

"It's a lifestyle for me," she says. "But we also do this in memory of Shaun and other family members that were cowboys and great men. We do it as a cowboy tradition."

"The horse is the only way to drive cattle," Wyatt says. "It's about feel. With a horse you can read and feel the pressure you are putting on the cows. With a quad or ATV it's harder to read and you end up pushing too hard."

Horses can also navigate the rocky bushes and narrow ravines better than anything motorized or human-made.

Wyatt kicks her horse and races to "pressure" a cow that has wandered away from the pack.

The drive passes by Area 27 Motorsports Park, an exclusive, membership-based luxury motorsports club. Its track winds across the land like a lounging snake. The *vrooom* of race cars chokes out the sound of the cowboys and braying cattle.

DAY THREE BEGINS with baking heat. Not a single cloud in the sky. The temperature will hit thirty degrees by 9:30 a.m. The ranch—where the cows are enclosed in a large pen—is quiet, save for the occasional *caw* of a raven and nicker and snort of a horse. This is desert heat. A yellow kind of oxygen that parches the back of the throat and rips the moisture from the skin.

The riders are shedding layers, dipping rags in water and tying them around their necks. Only dust kicked up from the hooves of horses and cows will shadow the convoy headed up the mountain today.

The procession, now 150 cattle strong, starts up a road. Cattle excrement lines the concrete, splattered across the yellow lines. Flies fill the nostrils of horses, and their heads knock up and down, straining at the reins. Riders swat the bugs off their arms and foreheads.

It's Brianna Stelkia's seventeenth birthday today, but she says she doesn't feel any older. Instead, she's frustrated because her horse is being disobedient.

Shaun was Brianna's cousin. He was also her friend. They used to lie on the floor and eat ice cream together while watching the TV show *Mantracker*. They also spent hours at the stables, where Shaun told Brianna all about the horses. She was too young to remember their names, but she'll never forget the day they carved "Shaun and Brianna" into clay rock, his steady hand guiding her words.

Shaun died when Brianna was nine. She goes quiet when people talk about him. And he's not the only friend she's lost. She also lost her cousin Leon. They used to haul horses together late into the night.

"I do this to honour Shaun and Leon," she says. "I need them to know I'm keeping the tradition going."

"Car!" she calls as a shiny Toyota mini SUV pulls up behind the herd. The cowboys scatter to the flanks and the vehicle slowly pulls its way through the mass of cattle.

The cattle don't want to climb uphill. Instead, they keep veering off the road. At one point they travel five hundred metres in the wrong direction. Turning them around will be impossible—cows won't go backwards.

The only option is to push them into the bush, across a creek and back onto the road. Tensions run high.

"C'mon cows. Get *moooving*," Brianna's voice cracks, exasperated, as she wades through the undergrowth on horseback, the thin branches of the trees pulling and snapping across her neck, forehead and arms, leaving behind red marks and scratches.

At last, the cows return to the highway. Brianna watches them, exhausted.

At times, the cows escape down sandy, steep banks where the horses are too tired or scared to go. Riders climb out of the saddle and slide down the banks on foot.

Eventually, around 1 p.m., clouds start to gather in the sky and the temperature drops. The air becomes more breathable, and the grass—now higher in the mountains—is no longer a wiry yellow but green. The ground is softer. The riders pass along the winding path of a forest, thick ponderosa pine on either side. A gushing creek is audible in the distance. Cows will survive a summer here.

At a seemingly random fork in the forest service road, riders receive word: the drive is finished.

The cows have found their greener pastures.

They extricate themselves from their saddles and load the horses into trailers attached to trucks. They slump onto the beds of the pickups, take off their hats and wipe the sweat from their foreheads. They light cigarettes as the truck reverses down the road.

The cows eat grass, drink water and watch as the riders pull away. The riders will return in the fall, ready to bring the cows—and their traditions—back down the mountain.

QUICK FACTS ABOUT THE OSOYOOS DESERT

- → The Osoyoos desert is located at the northernmost tip of the Great Sonoran Desert, a landscape that extends to Mexico. It includes Canada's warmest freshwater lake.
- → The surface of the desert is covered in a thin lichen crust that prevents soil erosion and holds trace amounts of water. It's home to eighty species found nowhere else in Canada.
- → Over the course of the twentieth century, sixty percent of its ecosystem was destroyed by vineyards, orchards, croplands and urban and industrial development. Only nine percent remains relatively undisturbed.

AGASSIZ

The Art of Growing Wheat in the Rain

CHRISTOPHER CHEUNG

(2020)

IT WAS THE NAME AGASSIZ that stuck out.

In 1972, Jim Grieshaber-Otto's parents, opposed to the Vietnam War, left the U.S. for a new life in Canada. As they drove through B.C., the Swiss-sounding name caught their attention. "My father's father was Swiss," says Grieshaber-Otto. The family stumbled upon a farm in Agassiz that had been put on the market the same day. "So they restarted their lives here when they were fifty."

As back-to-the-landers, the family aimed at self-sufficiency for the farm, which they called Cedar Isle.

While there are elements of a typical Canadian farm—the farmhouse, the barn, the gardens, the fields—there isn't the flatland horizon that one might associate with the golden fields of the Prairie provinces. Instead, the backdrop is the 2,100-metre peak of the majestic Mount Cheam, watching over this part of the Fraser Valley. At the edge of the farm are woods and a slough that flows into the nearby Fraser River.

"They had a milk cow, a flock of sheep, and they did spinning and weaving," says Grieshaber-Otto. "My mom made willow baskets, they made their own butter and cheese. We had beef cows as well."

The family grew their own oats and a bit of winter wheat, enough to feed the cows and chickens.

But the vast majority of B.C.'s grain isn't grown here. Rather, it comes from the Peace River region—mostly canola, but wheat, barley and oats as well. Agassiz's location, in the province's south and near the western coast, means challenging rains for such crops.

Grieshaber-Otto and his wife, Diane Exley, who met at the University of Reading while studying for their doctorates in agricultural botany, would eventually come to live and grow organic grain at Cedar Isle—and attract others curious about what's possible in this part of the province.

One of them was Yoshi Sugiyama, who grew up in Tokyo asking questions about food after a field trip to a nearby farm.

"We harvested the sweet potatoes," says Sugiyama. "I remember even drawing a picture of one after coming back. I really appreciated what a school in the middle of Tokyo tried to do, connect students to farming culture and farming heritage. I grew up very disconnected to what I ate. Everything came from the supermarket."

Moving to Vancouver in 1998 at age twenty-three, he became enamoured with the city's farmers' markets. He had no farming background, but the desire to be closer to food sources led him to volunteer on the University of British Columbia campus farm.

He was impressed by B.C. dairy and B.C. vegetables, but started to wonder about staples like grain. "It's the foundation of food," he says. "Civilization depends on it."

Looking for grain growers near the city, he found Cedar Isle in Agassiz, a small community of 6,300 people that most urbanites pass by on retreats to the nearby Harrison Hot Springs. From Vancouver, the farm is about an hour away. Sugiyama quickly became acquainted with the challenge of growing organic grains in a rainy place.

"It's risky, and grain is very unforgiving," he says. "The growing window is very limited. A late spring can delay the sowing time, and the harvest must happen before the rainy days. When Labour Day comes, it's like the weather turning off a switch: summer ends and fall arrives."

Around that time, others who came calling at Cedar Isle were the authors of *The 100-Mile Diet* and UBC students wondering if the farm could grow wheat for their Community Supported Agriculture program. The model gathers subscribers, essentially micro-investors, interested in getting a share of a local farm's harvest, whatever the results.

"How much do you want?" Grieshaber-Otto asked the students.

"Well, how much can you grow?" they responded.

At that point, the farm was only growing a few acres of wheat and oats for livestock. But the interest and the investment from the CSA led them to scale up and experiment.

"The people who buy the grains see the grain growing in the field, they see how it's processed in the barn, and they feel a part of it," says Grieshaber-Otto. "And what that CSA model initially did was give us enough money at the beginning of the year, so that we could finance the growing of the grain. So they were accepting some of the risk. If we had a crop failure, they knew they'd be out some money too. But that really gave us the ability to branch out and do a little bit of experimentation. We're like a little research station in a way."

One of their experiments grew "like magic": Skagit 1109, a hard, red winter wheat that came from the Washington State University's Breadlab in its pursuit to breed wheat suited to the local maritime climate.

"It sprouts and establishes in the fall and during the cold winter it gets snowed on, but it survives. And then in the springtime, because it's had a head start, it outgrows the weeds," says Grieshaber-Otto. "If you try and grow the stuff that grows in Saskatchewan, it often won't work."

Cedar Isle now grows twenty-six acres of wheat, oats and rye, thanks to the CSA model.

Come harvest season, the farm's decades-old machinery is put to use. One combine harvester is from the 1950s, a Massey-Harris, and the other is from the 1960s. There's an antique grain cleaner from the 1920s, which Grieshaber-Otto rescued from the Chilliwack dump and refurbished.

It takes a lot of shared knowledge to run an operation like this, and that's why farming is such a community effort, says Grieshaber-Otto. An artist friend renovated a combine that was gifted to the farm. Another friend of the couple helped rebuild a tricky gearbox, and located parts they later needed to fix their combine's clutch. And a master baker who used to teach at Vancouver Community College, who buys grain from the farm, was the one who helped crack the bread recipe for Skagit 1109.

These are the social connections that make it rewarding work, says Grieshaber-Otto.

After perusing farmers' markets for so long, Sugiyama ended up on the other side of the table. He introduces people to Cedar Isle's grains and some of the organic vegetables he grows on the land: cabbage, carrots, beets, leeks, daikon, winter kale and watermelon radish.

There's a huge market for them, with many Vancouverites of East Asian backgrounds curious about what culturally important produce with overseas roots can be grown in B.C. Many staples like bok choy and choy sum are "absolutely perfect" for our cool weather, he says. People have a growing appetite to follow the path of their food, as he once did.

"They want to find the source, a connection they can trust. Whenever I eat, I think about the people, from the farmers' market to the local bakery. We know them face to face."

Rather than the face of flour being a brand like Robin Hood, owned by multinational Cargill, farming grains means getting to know the people who mill and use them.

One of these people is Vadim Mugerman, who opened Bad Dog Bread in North Vancouver after tiring of his job in pest control.

"I like their growing philosophy," says Mugerman, who adds that the relationship is more important than what the labels and certifications of faraway organic grains might promise.

His first breads were so good that his girlfriend's rescue dog, Tommy, ate an organic loaf in minutes. It's a testament to Cedar Isle's quality that Tommy ate a bag of freshly milled flour the next day. The dog's appetite gave the bakery its name.

Before he returned to the family farm, Grieshaber-Otto worked in trade policy for the provincial government as well as the Canadian Centre for Policy Alternatives, where he worked on a report called *Threatened Harvest*, on protecting Canada's grain system.

"I spent years sitting in front of the computer, writing documents about sometimes really important stuff, such as the Water Protection Act or helping to stop bulk order exports from B.C.," he says.

But working on the farm, even with rainy days and the drudgery of winter months, has its rewards.

"One of the reasons I like growing wheat and oats is that it's going directly to people who really appreciate it. So much of what we do in life can seem abstract and isn't grounded in the soil."

QUICK FACTS ABOUT AGASSIZ

→ The TV show *Wayward Pines*, co-produced by M. Night Shyamalan and starring Matt Dillon, was filmed in Agassiz.

→ Agassiz is named after Lewis Nunn Agassiz, a relative of the Swiss biologist and geologist who discovered the megalodon and founded the study of glaciers and glaciology.

→ After a devastating flood destroyed the area's hop production in 1948, the community transitioned to corn, quickly becoming the corn capital of British Columbia.

ABBOTSFORD

The Blacker the Berry

HARRISON MOONEY

(2023)

I HAVE LONG BEEN RELUCTANT to speak generally on the experience of growing up in the Fraser Valley. Mine was not what one would call a universal upbringing. As a Black man, my experience is sure to differ from most of my Abbotsford brethren, but this includes other Black men. Adopted at eleven days by a white, evangelical family, I was brought up in defiance of the so-called Black experience, which I have had to discover of my own accord as an adult.

As a transracial adoptee, I have been burdened with the ultimate form of imposter syndrome: I am hardly representative of my own household. I would much rather speak for myself. Pressed to present *something* universal about my Fraser Valley childhood, however, I offer a bucket of blueberries.

For most of the year, blueberries are purchased in little plastic boxes from the Save-On-Foods, where you pay a pretty penny for a pittance of the local superfruit. But when the summer hits its zenith, blueberries seemingly fall from the sky, and in Abbotsford, where Costco is king, few can resist the great savings of buying in bulk. Before long, every household is saddled with a box or a one-gallon bucket—more than you'll ever be able to get

through before they go bad. Bake them into pies, eat them as sides, make syrups and compotes and jams. My brothers and I would eat huge bowls of blueberries swimming in milk with a spoonful of sugar for breakfast. It hardly makes a dent in the supply, and eventually any Abbotsford resident is bound to ask themselves the age-old question: *What am I going to do with all these blueberries?*

I never thought much about this inconvenient abundance until I started working for the *Vancouver Sun* about a decade ago, and found myself covering the multiple lawsuits and grievances launched by temporary foreign workers all throughout the rural region. The conditions for these labourers are brutal. Workplace health and safety violations are a constant—the shelters are cramped and inadequate, the machinery is outdated and dangerous—and if these issues are reported, they're deported, or at least replaced. They are, after all, not citizens. To these farms, they're a resource, and there's plenty more where these ones came from.

The resource is under-market labour, that linchpin of free enterprise. Temporary foreign workers often make less than the minimum wage, thanks in large part to discriminatory carve-outs in B.C. legislation. Blueberry-pickers, for instance, are excluded from labour protections surrounding guaranteed hourly salary, as well as guaranteed hours, time off and overtime pay, and while it seems anathema to say so, their labour seems akin to slavery.

A cursory look at post-slavery commerce makes clear that this labour force comes to the west in the aftermath of abolition. It's a straight line. Use the S-word, of course, and you'll be reminded that these workers are making some money. It's nowhere near the going rate for human beings in this region, as a matter of law, but it's *not slavery*. One imagines the money paid for their services is not so much for labour as for the right to deny that the slave trade persists. It is always more fiscally sound to live in denial about oppression than to do something about it.

This is the human condition in Abbotsford. Speaking more generally these days, I dare say that growing up in the resource-rich Fraser Valley is the experience of being wilfully blind to the inhumanity and exploitation that make such a life possible.

This is a significant theme of my 2022 memoir, *Invisible Boy: A Memoir of Self-Discovery*, which traces my life from infancy—the age of my adoption—to my mid-twenties, when I first reunited with my biological mother. During that first meeting, my mom asked me the same question many have posed: What was it like to grow up in Abbotsford? This time, rather than defer to others I deemed normal, I found myself consumed with providing an answer.

I wanted her to know me like a mom knows her son, to have context for who I became. The result was the memoir released this past fall after a gruelling, disorientating period of reflecting upon a truly traumatic childhood, and the subsequent mental health crisis I hope is just wrapping up now, with this essay, the first thing I've written since closing the book on my book.

I like to describe *Invisible Boy* as a journey from white cult to Black consciousness. It is the story of a lie unravelling before my eyes: the false narrative of being plucked from my mother's womb and miraculously inserted into a white family by the hand of God. Despite a lifetime of brainwashing and isolation, my path eventually leads to a face-to-face meeting with the actual architect of my existence—my biological mother—and a formal reckoning with the circumstances surrounding her decision to surrender me to strangers. She was sixteen then, a child of the B.C. foster system and a victim of so many abuses in provincial care that she was a cinch to coerce. She wanted to keep me, her handlers said no, and that was that. The fact is that mine was not so much an adoption as an abduction and this, not some Biblical maxim, was the truth that set me free.

AFTER THE BOOK was released, I received numerous messages from other transracial adoptees, many of whom were raised not far from me and led to believe, just as I was, that their experience was too singular to see any solidarity with anyone, especially other adoptees and people of colour. Like me, these adoptees had no idea of where to turn for kinship, camaraderie or the validation of their experience. We were all by ourselves.

One such adoptee, Abbotsford teacher Shayla Bird, is the founder of Black Connections, a group that seeks to remedy the isolation that so often accompanies Blackness in the Fraser Valley. Every Black high-school student was invited to join the fledgling group and most did, finding a safe space to share their experience, with the exception of a few kids whose parents balked, for fear that encouraging their children to see kinship in Blackness was akin to self-othering.

I'm very suspicious these days of any politic that opposes solidarity among Black folks. In my book, I joke that two's a crowd when you're Black, but it's not really a joke: this understanding is integral to Blackness all over this province, if not the whole country. In recent months, I've developed a friend group with several other Black fathers in Vancouver. We went out together one night, and the experience of walking down the street four Black men deep was so unusual that none of us could keep from saying something. Even in East Vancouver's Commercial Drive neighbourhood, we felt all eyes on us, and standing on the sidewalk near a bar, deciding where to go next, we were met by a hostess, who came all the way out to the curb just to ask, *Can I help you?*

It is not unusual to see Black folks in B.C. What's unusual is seeing Black folks in community, walking together, laughing together, simply *being* together. Many of us have been socialized, if not explicitly encouraged, to *not* do that, and it is maddening to learn that this mindset persists in my hometown.

Last winter, I performed a reading for the Black Connections group at Yale Secondary School, their home base.

The event was sold out, and I was stunned that night to meet so many people with lives that mirrored mine, down to the smallest of details. *Our experiences are so similar,* one woman said. *Even the little things. Your adoptive parents bought you a Toyota Echo and used it as a kind of emotional blackmail. My parents did that too—same make and model.* I met a man who looked just like me, but a decade older. He treated me like some kind of superhero. *I didn't think anyone would ever be able to tell my story,* he said. *I don't know how you did it.*

And so lately I have come to know that mine was not, after all, a life unlike anyone else's.

A FEW SUMMERS AGO, I brought my toddlers to the Birchwood Dairy Farm in Abbotsford—to my mind, still the best ice cream within driving distance of my house. Plus, they let you meet the cows. We returned to Vancouver with a bucket of blueberries, and while I can't quite remember deciding to buy one, I do recall staring at the massive white pail, which took up at least a quarter of my kitchen counter space, and wondering aloud for the first time since moving to Vancouver: *What am I going to do with all these blueberries?*

I put some in a salad for my mom, who visited my home for the first time since we met a decade earlier. My partner baked the customary pie. I ate a bowl for breakfast the next morning. But mostly, I found myself staring at all this abundance and thinking about the exploitation that made it possible for me to be overwhelmed by the food that I was scrambling to devour. Obsessed with my book then, I started to see myself in the one-gallon pail, just another commodity obtained with so little effort that there was nothing else to do but resent it for aging so quickly.

We mostly adopt babies and children, after all, those without the insight or perspective to quite understand what's been done to them. For years, these children can carry on believing that their owner is their parent, and shutting out the inconvenient truths about their lives. But then they mature. They grow into adults. They find language, grow consciousness, find each other, and soon they have enough information and experience to see the world for what it is, and what it means for their existence. For a good long while, the adoptive family can consume their blueberries however they choose. Eventually, though, the fruit goes bad.

I went bad. The last time I saw my adoptive mother, just before my book was published, I told her that my biological mom had died suddenly of leukemia a week or so prior. My mother said nothing, but as she was leaving, she offered a clinical, *I'm sorry about your mom*. It wasn't enough, but by then my grievance was so large, and my grief so overwhelming, that I can't imagine what else she could have said to offer comfort. We were so far apart by then. I'd been growing mould for years.

That was the same year that the flooding turned much of Abbotsford into a lake. At the time, much of the reporting drew attention to the fact that Abbotsford is *supposed to be* a lake, which was dredged in 1925 to make way for agriculture in the Sumas Prairie. This decision was met with near-unanimous approval, with just one note of dissent preserved in the historical record. "I am opposed to the dam because it will mean more starvation for us," said the Chief of the Sumas First Nation.

Needless to say, he was ignored and Sumas Lake no longer exists, except when the waters cannot be contained.

As another summer approaches, I'm dreaming about blueberries, and of the inconvenient abundance so typical to the Fraser Valley, an abundance made possible by exploitation and oppression.

I know that some will resist this comparison. Temporary foreign workers aren't slaves, and Black babies aren't blueberries. After all, it's obviously more significant to raise a child than to eat a bowl of fruit for breakfast. Fine. But from my perspective, it's really just a matter of degrees, and you know what they say: the blacker the berry, the sweeter the juice.

QUICK FACTS ABOUT ABBOTSFORD

→ With a census population of 153,524, Abbotsford is the second largest municipality in British Columbia.

→ Abbotsford-Mission is the most charitable metropolitan area in Canada. Residents donate a median $900 per year.

→ The city is home to the oldest surviving Sikh temple in the western hemisphere. Built in 1908, the Gur Sikh Temple was designated a National Historic Site on July 31, 2002.

SURREY

Tending the Fields of Resistance

DAVID P. BALL

(2021)

CÉSAR CHÁVEZ was already a legendary champion for farmworkers' rights in the United States when he arrived at David Thompson Secondary School in Vancouver on April 26, 1980, to mark what would prove to be a historic day.

Chávez co-founded the U.S. National Farm Workers Association in 1962, led boycotts and marches, went on hunger strikes and relentlessly organized to win higher pay and safer conditions in fields and factories.

Now he was here as a guest to celebrate the start of the Canadian Farmworkers Union, twenty days in existence. Its enemies had not waited to flex. Just ten days before, the home of the union's new vice-president, Jawala Singh Grewal, had been attacked by thugs who bashed in windows with baseball bats.

The dream had sprouted nineteen months before, when thirty farmworkers collected in a Surrey school to talk about how to change oppressive conditions they faced. And now five hundred had gathered to stand firm and celebrate a big step.

Chávez told them, "Although we're poor, let them never forget that although they have money, we have time. And there's never, ever so relentless an enemy as time when the time comes!"

Next to Chávez onstage that day was Charan Gill, then forty-three, with glasses and curly hair not yet turned snowy white. Gill was one of the visionaries of the Canadian Farmworkers Union and he would prove Chávez right—in his time, making an outsized mark on Canada's history by helping to win many battles against exploitation, hate and discrimination.

Gill not only unionized Canadian farm labourers, he founded a national anti-racism organization and built one of the most successful immigrant non-profits in the province.

When Gill died in February 2021 at the age of eighty-four, the outpourings were immediate. Many pointed out that his life represents more than one activist's legacy. He is at the heart of an epic story of generations of exploited immigrants in Canada who chose to risk much and fight back.

CHARANPAL SINGH GILL was born in Hong Kong and grew up in India, in the tiny village of Mahal Khurd, southwest of Ludhiana, Punjab. He lost his father at an early age and was raised with five brothers and sisters by his mother. He earned a master of arts in Punjabi language from Panjab University, then in his twenties returned to Hong Kong where he worked as a security guard in a bank, and as an editor at the *South China Morning Post* newspaper.

In 1967, his sister suggested he move to Canada, and so, with plans to put down roots and then send for his wife and children, he set off alone to B.C.

He found work in a sawmill in Williams Lake but injured his wrist and became a social worker in Prince Rupert. In 1969, he succeeded in bringing his family to join him, and in 1973, they moved to Surrey. It was a fertile place for both agriculture and activism.

"When my father came here to Canada, he saw there were a lot of people—especially immigrants—being exploited here," says Gill's son Paul. "People weren't getting their wages. They were getting injured. He said, 'We gotta do something about this.'"

Charan Gill possessed a charisma that helped make organizing easier. "To a lot of his friends, he was a big personality, but never overbearing. Just a guy everyone wanted to be around," his son says.

And opposing oppression was in his blood. Gill's grandfather, Baba Dulla Singh, had been heavily involved in the Ghadar cause—a revolutionary movement founded in 1913 by the South Asian diaspora in the U.S. and Canada to support ending British colonial rule in India. The movement gained followers in British-ruled Hong Kong and in Panama, where Singh dedicated years to rallying workers under the Ghadar banner.

Ghadar members were among those shot dead by British Indian troops in what was then known as Calcutta, after Canada turned away most would-be immigrants aboard the *Komagata Maru* and the vessel returned to India. The British claimed the Ghadars were using the ship to recruit.

At one point, the Soviets invited Singh to an international freedom fighter training school. One of his classmates reportedly was future Chinese communist leader Mao Zedong.

Charan Gill must be seen within the radical tradition of his grandfather and anti-colonial militancy, in the view of B.C. journalist Gurpreet Singh. "The Ghadars were a group of Indian rebels established to fight back against racism abroad and colonialism back home. Charan inherited a lot from his grandfather—a lot of his fight against racism and injustice—but he also had first-hand experience of racism when he came to Canada."

So the intergenerational saga of Gill's family includes anti-colonial rebels, revolutions, wartime occupations, political prisoners and exiles, and the century's great mass migration to find a better life overseas.

"All of us inherited this sense of justice and adventurous spirit," says son Paul. "The theme is independence, a 'don't tread on me' philosophy."

As B.C.-born Virginia Tech professor Bikrum Gill notes, Charan Gill also exemplifies "a certain history within our community of finding place, identity and belonging in Canada as a settler colony—not by fitting in, like a 'model minority,' but by contesting its exclusionary premise."

"Rights are not gifts from beneficent owners or employers," he adds. "They're won through struggles like Charan waged."

After mobilizing farmworkers, Gill helped organize largely racialized sectors, such as domestic workers and janitors. He was plenty used to battling bigotry, having co-founded the BC Organization to Fight Racism in November 1980, seven months after the launch of the Canadian Farmworkers Union.

At the time, Indo-Canadians were among people of colour most often violently attacked by racists. The organizer of the Western Canada chapter of the Ku Klux Klan claimed the group had two hundred members, and sought to open an office in Vancouver.

Gill found hate-filled graffiti on his property. He received death threats. He would not be deterred.

He went on to found and run until his 2017 retirement the Progressive Intercultural Community Services Society, a non-profit that today provides independent and assisted-living housing for seniors, a transition shelter for immigrant women, language lessons, tax clinics, immigration settlement services, job banks, youth training, a food bank and multicultural drug and alcohol counselling. In 1991, Gill and PICS developed a legal tool kit for agricultural labourers, translated into Punjabi, Spanish and Chinese. In 2004, they created Colony Farm, an organic sustainable agriculture training centre.

Farming remained close to Gill's heart throughout his life. Even when very old, he took pleasure in driving a tractor on his small family plot. Growing up, Paul remembers the family pitching in to work that land. It "was really homestead life," he says. Eventually, the homestead became a blueberry farm by virtue of "a small patch of really nice blueberries."

AFTER HIS INITIAL SPEECH at the launch of the Canadian Farmworkers Union forty-one years ago, César Chávez returned again and again to celebrate the barriers Charan Gill and others were knocking down in B.C.

Farmworkers were among the "worst-treated workers" in the province, notes Simon Fraser University labour historian Mark Leier, yet when Gill and others took up their fight it wasn't even legally clear they were allowed to unionize. The farmworkers union not only "looked after people as workers, but also as recent immigrants denied access to basic human rights."

Among Gill's fellow advocates was a young lawyer named Ujjal Dosanjh, who ended up becoming the thirty-third premier of British Columbia. He did so by getting elected leader of the BC New Democrats after his predecessor was forced to step down under a cloud of suspicion. It was Gill who talked Dosanjh into running, even though the party was wounded and doomed to be trounced in the approaching 2001 election.

What Dosanjh remembers his friend Gill telling him is this: "Look, you're brown and you have a good chance of winning the party leadership. We don't know when there will be a next time a non-white person will be in as good a position to be the leader. Do it not for yourself, but for all of the people who are going to look at you and say, 'I can be that too.'"

Gill and Dosanjh shared another bond—their opposition to the use of violent means in support of establishing a Sikh state of Khalistan independent of India. As outspoken moderates on the issue in B.C.'s Sikh community, Dosanjh was assaulted by a man with an iron bar and seriously injured in 1985, and a year later Gill was roughed up by fundamentalists at a temple.

Gill would not be silenced. Not even by age. One day, an elderly Gill showed up to address a rally for an Indian political prisoner. He looked out at the crowd and spoke through a megaphone with his characteristic charisma mixed with grit.

"Now I'm eighty-plus. And my knees do not work so well anymore," Gill declared. "So now is the time for youngsters to step forward."

QUICK FACTS ABOUT SURREY

→ In 2008, a day before she released her first studio album, *The Fame*, Stefani Joanne Angelina Germanotta played a show at Surrey's Mirage Nightclub for $25 a ticket. You might know Germanotta better as Lady Gaga.

→ Surrey is home to the man with the longest beard in the world, according to the *Guinness Book of World Records*.

→ Surrey's coat of arms includes a racehorse to symbolize Canada's third-largest rodeo, held in Cloverdale; a farm horse to represent the region's agricultural industry; and the Peace Arch, the landmark celebrating peace between the U.S. and Canada.

GRANVILLE ISLAND

Amidst the Tourists, Creating a "Landscape of Fear"

MICHELLE CYCA

(2022)

IF YOU OVERHEARD CHUCK DECOSTE talking about his job, you might get the impression that he works in a kindergarten classroom. He talks a lot about positive reinforcement, discouraging bad behaviours, and the importance of being a good caregiver.

But DeCoste doesn't work with kids. He's the Vancouver regional coordinator for the Raptors, a wildlife management and conservation organization, and spends his days communing with hawks, eagles and falcons.

You might spot him or one of his colleagues at BC Children's Hospital, chasing off nesting pigeons, or at Vancouver International Airport, preventing birds from flying into your airplane. (The Canada goose, incidentally, is the third-deadliest species when it comes to aircraft collisions.)

I first noticed them at Granville Island, where members of the Raptors team use hawks to chase away gulls and crows. From my counter seat in the market, facing False Creek, I watched as a man wearing a gauntlet—the thick leather glove worn by a falconer—lifted his arm to meet a brown bird, roughly the same size as a typical seagull, which I now know is called a Harris's

hawk. It was hard to tell whether they were performing or working as they posed agreeably for photos with curious tourists.

But then I noticed something else. The people eating outside in the crisp fall air seemed cavalier, carefree, not at all concerned that a crow or seagull might swoop over their shoulder at any moment in pursuit of french fries. I grew up going to Granville Island, which gets eight to ten million visitors a year. As a kid, I understood that a bird stealing your lunch was a rite of passage and a lesson in situational awareness. Now those avian Artful Dodgers were nowhere to be found. The keen-eyed brown bird was not just a magnet for selfies; it had also transformed the environment.

GRANVILLE ISLAND is not really an island. "It's mudflats and a sandbar," says Tom Lancaster, the general manager. Built over a century ago as an industrial site, it once housed nothing but mills and factories; there was no green space on the island at all until the 1970s. And while some of the original tenants are still operating on the island, including the cement plant (famous for its cheerfully painted seventy-foot-tall silos) and a steel fabricator, it's also become a quasi-natural space that almost looks like it was always part of the landscape.

"What we have now is a dumbed-down version of that interface with nature. We have trees planted on this artificial island, and those are now home to birds and squirrels," says Lancaster. "But there's no way to peel back the layers and imagine what this place looked like three hundred years ago." In its artificiality, it inhabits a kind of paradox: close to nature but not of it.

Still, each year it brings visitors and residents into close contact with the many species who live there—"lots of birds, squirrels, raccoons, occasionally a coyote, and many rodents," according to Lancaster, who adds that rats have been largely evicted. ("Once you get a large enough mouse population, they actually chase the rats away.") In the water, visitors can spot harbour seals and otters dining on herring and anchovies—two fish species that have returned to False Creek in recent years as a result of habitat restoration.

The proximity to nature is part of Granville Island's singular appeal, but it can also lead to problems. In 2021, a family of river otters took up residence, tunnelling under the island to build their dens and causing a sinkhole. "Which is the only reason we found out about them," says Lancaster.

Another problem, of course, is the food-snatching birds. "You would normally see raptors in the wild feeding on seagull eggs, keeping things in check," Lancaster says. "But there's no predator-prey balance here at all. In some ways, the seagulls are the predators now. They'll prey on anyone with a bagel in their hands."

Bringing the Raptors to the island restores a simulacrum of natural order—and it also shifts how humans and animals coexist on the island.

A hundred years ago on Granville Island, Lancaster says, people didn't want to work with nature at all. The idea was to fight hard against it and tame it. "We imposed ourselves on an environment that was stewarded by Indigenous peoples long before settlers arrived," he says. And yet, as a tunnelling family of river otters occasionally reminds us, nature is resilient. Animals adapt to human trickery, which gives a program like the Raptors an advantage.

"Wild birds don't habituate to the presence of our raptors, because they're real predators," says DeCoste. "If you look at the United States, they're still using things like firearms to clear birds from that sky. So let's say you shoot six ducks—the next six who pass through aren't going to learn any lessons from that. But when we put a falcon up in the sky, ducks are flying by and seeing that there is a predator in the air, so they start avoiding the area."

Over time, the birds are conditioned to avoid places like the airport and Granville Island. The Raptors website cheerfully describes this practice as "creating a landscape of fear."

The Raptors use different species for different purposes. Harris's hawks, whose natural range extends from the southwestern United States to South America, are particularly well-suited to Granville Island. The ones used by the Raptors are born in captivity; they don't take birds from the wild.

"Size-wise, they're between a crow and a raven," says DeCoste. "But they're the only true social raptor species in the world. They're a pack animal. So ours are really well-socialized, and they can be somewhere like [Granville Island] without getting stressed out. They're really friendly and totally at home here."

Choosing the right bird for the job is an art. "I compare it to golf—you need the right club," says DeCoste.

This observation presents an excuse to segue into a delightful tidbit of etymological trivia. "Actually, the word *caddy* is an old falconry term, which used to be *cadge*," DeCoste says. "Back in the day, kings or queens would have a falconer who would train all their birds, and when they hunted, the cadge would have this cool portable perch with all these different birds sitting around them. Depending on the quarry, the cadge would pick the right bird for the job. And that's what we do."

At the airport, the Raptors team uses eagles and falcons to chase birds away from aircraft. "I work a lot with Hercules—he's a bald eagle, and he's my big, beautiful baby boy," says DeCoste. "We use him primarily to deter snow geese, because they react powerfully to bald eagles, who are their natural predators."

At Granville Island, DeCoste says, the primary goal is keeping birds away from human food—which is good for them too. When birds have access to human food and trash, it inflates their populations, making them more susceptible to pandemics and disease. Human food and trash are also higher in nitrates—meaning the birds' feces is too, which can cause algae blooms in the lakes where they hang out.

This prompts me to ask DeCoste a follow-up question: Aren't the raptors tempted by the bagels and heaps of garbage too? DeCoste, sounding like a kindergarten teacher again, says it's all about giving positive reinforcement and keeping your cool.

Let's say one of the birds decides it wants to go snack on food from the face of the landfill, DeCoste says. "That's just a hawk being a hawk: it sees food, it wants it, it eats it. You can't blame the bird."

"Instead, you have to take a hard look at what your co-workers are doing, so you can figure out how to shift his focus to something else. Maybe you fly him further from the garbage, or maybe you offer him more tidbits. We give them a lot of chicken and quail—we try to keep their diets as close to their natural diet as possible," DeCoste says.

He admits falcon training is not an easy skill to teach. "So much of it is based on feel. You're learning the body language of the bird. It's not like learning how to use a skill saw, which is going to act the same way every time you plug it in and press a button. You need to learn to make relationships, and just like making relationships with people, there's no formula that works every time. You're learning to open yourself up to a bird, to watch and pay attention, to make them comfortable. So much of our job is about positive reinforcement, so that when a bird goes flying and you ask them to come back, they choose to come back."

Once you've established that bond, the job is simple: let the raptor do what they were born to do—watch it fly around and have fun rebuffing other birds, feed it lots of rewards, and make sure it's happy.

For DeCoste, developing relationships with his avian colleagues has been the best part of the job—particularly the bond he has with Hercules. "When I started this job, I was actually reluctant to work with a predator that big," DeCoste admits. "They're daunting. They're so strong. They absolutely have the capacity to hurt you. But the surprising thing has been the richness and depth of the relationship that I've formed with him, and just seeing that these birds are more than scary predators. They actually have these really amazing personalities and can be quite sweet." Hercules, DeCoste says, likes to play fetch as much as any playful Labrador.

Back on Granville Island, Tom Lancaster says the success of the raptor program speaks for itself. "It tells a story, and it's educational," he says. "People are exposed to something they'd never have seen otherwise."

Lancaster just hopes that people can learn to adapt their behaviour too. "We have signs up all over the island, and yet we still see people feeding the birds," he says. "When we do, we gently go over to them and take the opportunity to explain that feeding wildlife is inherently dangerous, and just a bad thing to do."

But the practice persists. "People think, 'I have a bird feeder at home—why shouldn't I feed these birds?'" Lancaster says.

The Raptors have demonstrated that even a seagull can learn to adjust when presented with an appropriate deterrent. Maybe humans could benefit from being chased by a falcon every once in a while too.

QUICK FACTS ABOUT GRANVILLE ISLAND

→ This human-made island originally comprised two sandbars that vanished and reappeared with the tides. Salish peoples used the area for fishing, catching shellfish and gatherings. The now thirty-six-acre island was completed in 1916 by using fill dug up from the bottom of False Creek.

→ During the Great Depression, the island was home to squatters who subsisted on fishing, foraging and selling supplies to nearby businesses.

→ Granville Island was originally named Industrial Island, after the hotbed of sawmills, ironworks and slaughterhouses that populated its streets. During World War II, its factories, staffed by women, manufactured defence equipment.

VANCOUVER

Dumplings for a New Year

FIONA TINWEI LAM

(2014)

ACCORDING TO REFERENCE BOOKS about Chinese holidays, the dumplings that are served around Chinese New Year are good luck because they resemble gold ingots. I've never been anywhere near a gold ingot, but there's something very satisfying about biting into the crispy golden bottoms of freshly made dumplings. For me, it's not Thanksgiving or Christmas feasts with my family that I remember most from my childhood, but the times we made dumplings together for Chinese New Year.

My widowed single mother was a busy physician struggling to make ends meet, so she didn't often have time to make a slow-cooked meal from scratch. When we weren't going out for fast food, we had all kinds of convenience foods from the cupboard or freezer at our fingertips. I learned how to shake and bake, microwave frozen mixed vegetables, make dip out of dried onion soup mix, whip up casseroles with canned mushroom soup, and stir the correct proportions of margarine and milk into the neon-orange no-name imitation Kraft Dinner. We usually ate our supper in fifteen minutes, often with little or no conversation, and then dispersed afterwards to our rooms or the TV room. The years following my father's death were difficult for all of us. My mother was often

overwhelmed and exhausted. I was withdrawn and confused, unable to comfort my younger siblings or even myself.

There were occasions, however, when my mother had the time and energy to cook—sometimes a stew, a roast, or Ann Landers's famous meat loaf (made in bulk). She'd rarely cooked Chinese food, having never learned to cook while growing up in Hong Kong in a large household. The number of courses and the amount of preparatory chopping and marinating involved in Chinese cuisine were daunting. But once a year, she would haul out a thick Chinese cookbook and we'd join her in the kitchen to help out. I'd wash down the table while she'd go over the ingredients and methodology.

First, she chopped up cabbage and put the chunks through a manual grinder. She added ground pork to the bowl of shredded cabbage, splashed in some seasonings and blended everything together with bare hands. In another bowl she mixed flour and water together, and when the proportions were just right, she started kneading, transforming the paste into a muscular dome of dough. She tore off a wad, kneaded it down to a disk, rolled it in flour, then cranked it through an old pasta machine. Side by side, my sister and I took cookie cutters to cut circles out of the dough as it unfurled before us. Our mother gathered the scraps to re-roll and for us to re-cut, tossing a few lumps for our little brother to play with until he was old enough to join us at the dumpling assembly line.

In between cranking out the runners of dough, my mother stuffed the circles with the perfect amount of filling, crimping the edges together swiftly and expertly in a way I could never imitate. When the rows of dumplings packed the trays, she moved to the stove, boiling half of the dumplings and frying the other half. The sounds of bubbling and sizzling filled the kitchen. Meanwhile, we washed the table and our hands for the finale: the steaming pillows of dough as well as the crisp ones that glistened with oil. Almost as soon as they hit the serving plate, we dove in, dipping them in soy sauce and vinegar before devouring them. The second batch also zoomed from mouth to throat to belly. By the third batch, we were munching more thoughtfully, the edges of hunger and anticipation smoothed away. Finally, we sat back in our seats, sated and dazed.

YEARS LATER, I found out that our use of a pasta machine and cookie cutters wasn't typical. Traditionally, this dumpling dough is fashioned into a long cylinder with small chunks sliced off and deftly rolled into a circle with a small rolling pin. When I first saw this process in a local noodle house, I marvelled at the speed and dexterity of the cooks just as I'd marvelled at my mother's earlier. Somehow this ordinary process seemed almost magical. When I became a mom myself, I brought my son to watch the dumplings being made. He perched on a chair beside other fascinated kids, while the chefs looked up occasionally to smile.

Like the kids pressed up against the glass, I still find a strange comfort in watching experienced hands create morsel after perfect morsel. I often feel the same way witnessing anyone doing any activity with great skill and pride in craftsmanship. In those overlooked niches of our everyday existence, there must be so many tiny moments of beauty where a human does or creates something with such ease that it seems as natural as breathing. It doesn't have to be as complex as an Olympic skater doing a triple toe loop or a classical pianist playing Liszt. It can be a mechanic fixing an engine, a baker making a pie, a tailor repairing a torn seam, or a doctor delivering a baby (something I wish I could have witnessed my mother do while she was still practising).

Think of that saying "You're in good hands." It means that you can let go of worry, and feel assured that you're with someone who knows what they are doing, who can take care of what needs to be dealt with, who will guide, advise or even protect you when you are feeling vulnerable in this crazy, unpredictable universe. My mother's competent, confident hands delivered babies, sewed sutures, created art, played music and also made delicious dumplings. When we made them with our mother, my siblings and I knew we were in good hands.

THE TIME WHEN I could lift my son onto my shoulders so he could see the dragons and lions cavorting in the Chinese New Year parade in Chinatown is long past. He was born in the Year of the Horse, in 2002. In 2014, as I write the first iteration of this essay, he can now almost lift me; he's also reached the age I was when I started making dumplings with my mother, when she let me move past cutting out dough circles and into filling more than a token few.

My son has made dumplings with me before, albeit with pre-cut dough circles from a Chinese mall in Burnaby. Our stripped-down dumpling-making doesn't match the grand, floury productions of my childhood, and I still can't crimp the edges of my dumplings the way my mother could.

But there's something from those few times when we cooked together as a family that persists today when I cook with my son—a sense of satisfaction that comes with making food that will nourish ourselves and others, and the pleasure of a cultural tradition being passed on, one he will be able to share with the significant people in his life during the many Chinese New Year celebrations to come. Perhaps more importantly, it's a way for me to pass on a story to him about his grandmother, and how, during those brief, sporadic but magical times, she bound us together as a family.

MORE QUICK FACTS ABOUT VANCOUVER

→ Every single eastern gray squirrel in Stanley Park is said to be the descendant of eight pairs of squirrels gifted to Vancouver by New York in 1909 (oops).

→ The city's most elected mayor—L. D. Taylor, elected nine times from 1919 to 1933—was an American.

→ The Vancouver fire of June 1886, which took place two months after incorporation, destroyed the city within one hour.

VANCOUVER

Elegy for a Building Manager

STEVE BURGESS

(2020)

JOANNE WAS OUR BUILDING MANAGER. She was also my closest neighbour—our doors face each other at the end of the third-floor hallway. Last week another neighbour knocked on my door and told me Joanne was dead. There was no lead-up, no warning. It may as well have been a lightning strike.

This has been a year of death. The first global pandemic in a hundred years has ensured that the ultimate talking point has been a constant in the public conversation. Every night the evening news leads off with death tolls. It's been like wartime without the censorship.

And yet anything seen on the news offers a comforting degree of separation. Most of us are dealing only with the pandemic's secondary effects. It's a struggle to be grateful for that—the restrictions and precautions have been a pain in the ass, and for those lucky enough to have avoided a direct experience of death and grief, keeping it all in perspective has been rather like hearing Mom say, "There are starving children in the world. Eat your creamed spinach."

Jo didn't die of a Covid-related cause. Recently diagnosed with a serious illness, she kept the news to herself, was admitted to hospital, and quickly suffered a fatal

stroke. She was fifty-five years old, younger than me. Also more energetic, capable and competent. In fact, Joanne was hyper-competent. She was one of those people who quietly make the world run, down here at ground level. She ran our building, and five others, with an iron fist in a velvet glove. And the glove was removable. Mess around and find out.

Joanne and I bonded over our shared provincial roots, being the only sort of people who will go to Manitoba in December on purpose. She was a force of nature, and busy as she was, her closest hallway neighbour derived the greatest benefit from her industry. Her efforts show up around my apartment. It starts at the door. Jo liked to decorate hers with seasonal garlands and trinkets. "No one can see your door from the elevator," I told her. "You should decorate my door too. Get more exposure that way."

So she did. Like hers, my door would boast a butterfly for spring, a dragonfly for summer, a string of coloured leaves for autumn, a Christmas wreath. My bath mat is a Joanne discard, my big bottle of hand soap a hand-me-down after she found the lemon scent overpowering, my extra vacuum bags sourced by Jo since I couldn't find the right kind. My microwave came from a nearby alley. Joanne, knowing I needed one, alerted me to its presence. This microwave replaced an earlier one, picked up from a different alley after another Jo tip. She knew I wouldn't be too proud to grab a free back-alley appliance. Similarly, I came home one day a few months back to find a box of Trader Joe's maple granola outside my door, left behind by a neighbour who had moved out. Yes, it was past its expiration date, but not by much. Not everyone would welcome a box of fancy expired cereal, but Jo understood her people. "You know your market," I emailed her.

The cereal had a touching aspect as well. I chose to think of it as a peace offering. Last summer, after years of cheerful co-existence, I had poked the bear. Seeking to get my old car back on the road, I had borrowed a laundry room mop to wash off the dust. I didn't ask permission. And I dripped water in the lobby. She was incensed. This was the other side of Jo, occasionally glimpsed—the domestic Napoleon, fearsome in her rage and not inclined to let the small stuff slide. Hyper-competence has its dark side.

Joanne was a private person. Of course, we couldn't know the whole of her life. But maintaining boundaries is tough when you spend weekends at the office surrounded by, in effect, clients. Hers was the ultimate work-from-home job—our homes were her job. She did her best to draw the line. If you knocked on her door on a Saturday, the building damn well better be on fire.

In recent months some of my neighbours and I had seen more of those angry outbursts from her. It's a tribute to Jo that our typical reaction, following the initial indignation, tended to be concern. Was it burnout? Something else? We didn't know and still don't. We are just left with an absence.

Few people hope for a lingering death. But I have always been cognizant of its advantages. Think of Gord Downie. What a death the Tragically Hip singer had. A national tour. A televised concert event. So long, everybody! Thanks for all the love! You couldn't ask for a better send-off.

Then there is a case like Joanne's. Her story ended like *The Sopranos*: boom, black screen. Done. You are forced to grope back through your memories to recall your last interaction and hope it went okay. There's no chance to celebrate a life well-lived, especially in this no-funeral era.

One of my neighbours tells me that Covid has been almost a PTSD situation for his gay friends, bringing back the days when the spectre of AIDS haunted an entire community, in some cases inspiring episodes of irrational behaviour and finger-pointing that seem to be back in style. A lot of people soldiering through this war well recall the last one.

Then, too, the pandemic is running concurrently with the fentanyl crisis that is killing more of us here than coronavirus. And that's in addition to the general toll common to any month of the calendar. Following Jo's death, I discovered that our residential administrator (Jo's boss) lost her husband last month, and moreover that the head office had suffered the passing of several staff members, none of the deaths Covid-related. 2020 has been difficult, but the brutal message from our West End address has been that every year is a year of death. Every year is a time to grieve.

"In my practice, most of the people I see are dealing with their own feelings about loss," says Barb Crosby, a registered clinical counsellor based in Vancouver. "The onslaught of Covid news continually reminds them of death, sickness, inability to see their elders in care homes and fear for their own safety. Many are down and some depressed and anxious. I try to help them focus on resiliency. Maybe Viktor Frankl said it best: 'Everything can be taken from a [person] but one thing, the last of human freedoms—to choose one's attitude in any given set of circumstances, to choose one's own way.'"

I don't believe in ghosts. But it seems to me that we non-believers rarely acknowledge the bittersweet aspect of our skepticism. I would love to be visited by my late mother's spirit, have even secretly hoped for it. Now it seems strange that Joanne could leave her domain so abruptly and with such finality. Surely she still has things to do. Skeptic or not, I am going to keep an eye out for unexplained fixes—taps that stop dripping, leaks that dry up, loose towel racks that remain firmly, mysteriously in place.

Shamefully, it has crept into my mind that I could get away with some stuff now that I would never have attempted last month. I could borrow any number of mops. I could leave pools of water in the lobby and escape justice. But no. Even if I don't believe her avenging shade might come for me, such impulses must be resisted. We who remember Joanne must honour her with our courtesy and adherence to the laws of neighbourliness.

Just before leaving for the hospital, Joanne had put up a Christmas tree in the lobby. A champion decorator (Halloween, Valentine's, St. Patrick's Day, any excuse to deck the lobby), she did not get the chance this year. Someone posted a notice suggesting we decorate the tree in her memory.

I have a wooden ornament that my dad made a few months before he died, covered with blue lacquer and sporting a sprig of holly. I'd never had a chance to hang it before, since I never stay home in Vancouver for Christmas. Dad's ornament is on Joanne's tree now. I'll be around too. Nothing is quite the same this year.

QUICK FACTS ABOUT VANCOUVER

- When it comes to total tonnage moved in and out, the Port of Vancouver is the largest port in the country—in fact, it's larger than the next five Canadian ports combined.
- Botox was invented in Vancouver.
- Stanley Park is ten percent larger than New York's Central Park and is home to roughly half a million trees.

RICHMOND

The Golden Village at the Edge of the Ocean

CHRISTOPHER CHEUNG

(2023)

THE CUSTARDY SMELL of pineapple buns is in the air before the sun rises over the city of Richmond. The many malls of the Golden Village are waking up, the bakers cooling their first loaves of milk bread, the grocers unpacking their leafy greens and air-freighted lychees, the meat shops roasting the first pigs of the day in their ovens, filling the empty hallways with the smell of blistering skin.

When morning arrives, the Golden Village lives up to its name, the warm light washing over the landscape of shopping centres, drive-throughs and auto shops. In the parking lot of Parker Place mall, a colourful mosaic shrine to a four-faced Buddha stands tall among the Hondas and Mercedes-Benzes, glittering in the sun. At its base, people have left fruit, flowers and joss sticks, their smoky incense reminding passersby that this is not your average North American suburb.

Marquee signs rise up from the plazas on both sides of No. 3 Road, towering above the traffic like Roman columns. They announce everything from ginseng, dim sum and accounting services to commercial equipment for East Asian restaurants in both English and Chinese—a common sight everywhere in the Golden Village, Richmond, and beyond.

For over three decades, the broad expanse of the Pacific Ocean has become a highway for people zipping back and forth between East Asia and this Canadian city, where they've been putting down roots: white-collar and blue-collar workers, homemakers, transnational teens and seniors retiring in the West. This traffic has always been about push—for example, the pressures caused by China's growing might—and pull, in the allure of a stable future.

Calvin is part of the latest wave of people who left Hong Kong for Canada, many of them young and worried about the government's continuing crackdown on democratic freedoms. A former civil servant, he'd kept the thought of leaving at the back of his mind ever since his home city rolled out so-called national security legislation to eliminate dissent. When he finally decided to go, he packed his bags in a hurry.

"I took off for Vancouver days later," he says. "I decided to come first as a tourist and worry about the visa later. Right now, a lot of us who've just arrived are at supermarkets and restaurants, rather than continuing our former careers."

Calvin found it surreal to explore Richmond, with place names like Aberdeen and Admiralty borrowed from his home city—but with a slight lag.

"It's like Hong Kong—but in the '90s!"

EGYPT HAS ITS PYRAMIDS. Europe its churches. Neighbouring Vancouver has its signature glass towers.

In the 1990s, Richmond began building its own pyramids: a unique brand of mall that was a collision of urban Asia and suburban North America.

Emigration from East Asia had already started in the 1980s, bringing well-to-do families who were ready to settle into their own Canadian cul-de-sac.

Richmond, at the mouth of the Fraser River, was known as a farming and fishing community, with its fair share of attractive subdivisions. But the city transformed when deep-pocketed tycoons with colourful resumés crossed the Pacific to build a new vision of suburbia.

The first was Thomas Fung, the eldest son of legendary Hong Kong share trader Fung King Hey. Fung had a creative streak, launching the Saint Germain chain of bakeries and financing movies like the British war film *The Wild Geese*, starring Roger Moore. But, like his father, he was also active in the world of business.

In 1989, Fung unveiled his Aberdeen Centre. The name, of Scottish origin, comes from a harbour community in Hong Kong. The dream was for a multicultural mall, evenly split between eastern and western offerings, but North American franchisers weren't interested.

As a result, Aberdeen became an early example of the diasporic Asian mall, with traditional fare like dried seafood as well as contemporary offerings like a bowling alley and movie theatre, showing the latest Hong Kong action flicks.

A sculpture of Hong Kong's shard-like Bank of China Tower, the original designed by starchitect I. M. Pei, jutted out from the roof like a beacon of change.

Other wealthy players circled the area.

Among them was Kazuo Wada, of the successful Japanese supermarket and department store chain Yaohan. He built a Richmond mall to add to his expanding overseas collection.

And then there was Jack Lee, a Vancouver food distributor, who joined forces with a food conglomerate from his native Taiwan to build the President Plaza mall. It boasted a Buddhist temple and school above the multi-storey parking lot and one of the first T&T supermarkets. T&T, spearheaded by Lee's wife, would go on to become the country's largest Asian grocer.

Fung went on to build Parker Place, with the four-faced Buddha, and demolish his own Aberdeen Centre, which stood for only a little over a decade, erecting two new Aberdeen malls in its place.

These ornate malls rose up like castles, seeding new condos and plazas and restaurants and shops in the streets between. Professionals from doctors to insurance brokers, engineers to mechanics launched businesses catering to Cantonese and Mandarin speakers. Language schools opened to keep the young generation fluent. Congregations at Chinese churches swelled. Chefs brought their wide-ranging mastery, making working-class fare like congee, East-meets-West fusion at cha chaan tengs, and upscale seafood dishes at banquet halls.

After this period of heated development, what was once a landscape of light industry by the Fraser River emerged at the turn of the millennium as the Golden Village.

"WE, THE NEW VISIBLE MINORITIES, are experiencing exclusion."

So began a 2014 story in the *National Post* quoting Richmond residents who thought it was all too much: Chinese language on buildings, Chinese language on signs, Chinese language on ads.

"I want my community back," said a source described as a "lifelong Richmondite."

"I firmly believe that Chinese-only signs only serve to exclude the rest of the community and this is very un-Canadian," said another.

"This is about self-segregation," added a city council candidate. "Many people who come to Richmond decide that they don't want to integrate. I believe that they're cheating themselves out of a much more enriched life."

After the world wars and the years that Canada banned Chinese immigration, there were still flare-ups of anti-Asian xenophobia in the Vancouver region. Some echoed old fears of invasion, such as Chinese foreigners buying up real estate and Chinese students crowding white locals at school. Some were bizarre, such as Vancouver food inspectors cracking down on barbecue shops in the 1970s, claiming that their char siu was kept at inappropriate temperatures.

Joining those flare-ups was the issue of Chinese language signs in 2010s Richmond.

These signs of the times were diagnosed as the "canary in the coal mine" by two university geographers asked by the city to look into the tensions. Those who held tightly on to Canada's English and French nationhood viewed prominent Chinese-ness as part of that persistent "invasion narrative," they concluded.*

The city had enough sense not to come down hard on business owners with Chinese-only signs, finding that they only comprised three percent of total commercial signs and that the issue was "inflated by a small number of individuals."

The City of Richmond has rolled out rosy-sounding campaigns like its Cultural Harmony Plan and its Hate Has No Place campaign, initiatives that try to build cross-cultural connections, help immigrants and tackle racism and discrimination.

But these xenophobic worries still surface in the city, from racialized news coverage about how foreign buyers of real estate are turning Richmond into a "ghost city" to comments in Facebook groups from long-time locals lamenting the "good ol' days."

The city has been "destroyed," they say, with "nothing left but memories." In a group called Richmond Rants, Raves & Rapport, some complain about Chinese businesses being racist to white customers. "Do they not serve people like us?" a woman wrote about a restaurant that ran out of menus. "Racism is on the rise in Canada," someone added. Even the local rabbit rescue has

* geog.ubc.ca/news/considering-the-so-called-richmond-signage-issue/

encountered its share of racism, with passersby questioning visibly East Asian volunteers about whether they are going to eat them.

Then there are the full-throated racists, occasionally caught on camera. In a coffee shop during the pandemic, a man who allegedly threw a cup of coffee at the manager was caught on video saying, "Fuck you, Chinese," and "Coronavirus is you." At a train station, a man approached two women speaking Chinese and told them, "You're in Canada now. Why do we have to bend over backwards?"

DESPITE THESE TENSIONS, newcomers built up a unique multicultural and transnational community in Richmond.

It might not have the name recognition of Vancouver, but realtors in the 1990s joked with their clients about *Richmond* sounding like "Rich Man." Plus, for those familiar with Chinese mythology, there's the added auspiciousness of the city, an island in the middle of the river, looking a bit like a pearl in the mouth of the dragon-shaped surrounding land.

For Queenie Lai, the main mall in her life was Yaohan, where her mother had a salon. "We got to know all the other shop kids and would play with them after school," she says. Outside of mall life, Richmond meant studying Cantonese with a private tutor and acting in a local theatre group, performing in legends like *Mulan* and historical fare like a play based on the life of Dr. Sun Yat-sen. In her university years, she worked a co-op job in Hong Kong, where locals were wowed by her Cantonese fluency.

Ken Lam's main mall was the original Aberdeen. "It felt like a second home to my parents," who brought him to catch movies, he says. The food courts of the Golden

Village, almost all run by mom-and-pops, served homey meals and also nostalgic snacks from the bustling streets of Hong Kong, like bubble waffles and saucy rice rolls with mini siu mai. "My parents would always order the one drink: red bean with ice cream. My dad remembered drinking that as a kid."

For Kitty Tang, her mother found community and fitness in a mall. Immigrant seniors retiring in Richmond can find the experience isolating, but many have found friendships by hanging out in food courts over chess, newspapers and milk teas.

The lively use of space has spilled over to the non-Asian mall too, the one with the White Spot, the Sephora, the Abercrombie & Fitch. For almost three decades, a tai chi group with hundreds of members got permission from Richmond Centre to practise in its galleria before the shops opened—a perfect workout spot for the senior population. "No need to worry about rain, snow or wind," says Tang, who heard about the group from a neighbour before bringing her mother to exercise and joining it herself.

The mall's tai chi master, who taught the group until he was ninety-nine, once practised in pocket parks under the shade of trees and high-rises in Hong Kong. Shopping centres like these are, by nature, commercial spaces—but people adapted them into the public squares like those in the communities they left behind.

EMIGRANTS LIKE CALVIN don't know when they'll see their families again.

Heiky Kwan is among the locals of Hong Kong background helping to get them adjusted. She's at Vancouver

International Airport in Richmond regularly to pick up newcomers she's never met and take them out for dim sum and Costco runs.

"It feels fulfilling, but heavy," says Kwan. Unlike previous waves of newcomers, who've had months—even years—to plan their exits, many have never been to Canada before and are coming as quickly as circumstances allow. "Helping this community means that we're dealing with a lot of trauma."

Rev. Joshua Chow has seen his congregation at Koinonia Evangelical Church grow rapidly, something they've paved the way for by conducting online services in Hong Kong's time zone for those planning to make the move.

"We see a lot of whole families coming together. It's a very brave action," he says. "Some of the parents, they have very well-paid jobs in management in big companies, and when they come here, they do not have any expectation to find the same level of job. They really want to do the best thing for the next generation, so this is why they can make such a big decision, leave everything behind, to start over again."

There is also a group who grew up in Canada, returned to Hong Kong and are coming back. It's led geographers to come up with new terms to describe them, from *circular migrants* to *post-return migrants*.

In other words, Richmond isn't just a suburb of Vancouver—it's also now, in some ways, a suburb of East Asia, with an ocean-wide commute. With half the population identifying as ethnically Chinese, newspapers have taken to calling Richmond the most Chinese city in North America.

WHEN THE SUN SETS on Richmond, it's not quite dinnertime yet. It's when midnight approaches that Richmond really gets hungry. Tidy Christians from evening fellowships and sweaty badminton players wearing racquet bags are out in the Golden Village, looking for a bite to eat.

The food courts have closed, but Alexandra Road is alive. Its nickname in Chinese: "Eat Street." Students drive by in their growling supercars, showing off their outrageous spoilers, vibrant paint jobs and stickers with Pokémon and anime schoolgirls. The streets are bathed in the colourful glow of LED lightboxes, advertising everything from sushi to hot pot. Food couriers wearing smart teal vests zip in and out of restaurants, off to deliver noodles and grilled skewers to those wanting the offerings of the strip without venturing into its hustle and bustle. Decades of migration from Hong Kong, Taiwan and China mean that baked spaghetti, chicken steaks fried in tapioca batter, and whole fish with pickles in peppercorn oil are all represented here.

For the young people who've grown up in Asian metropolises, it's still too quiet. They call the city a "village," and not in an endearing way.

Still, they make do with what's available. If it's entertainment they're after, there are private rooms for mahjong and karaoke open until 2 a.m. Or they can eat and drink again. The seniors prefer the 24/7 McDonald's, where they can sip a cheap coffee. There's also fancier fare like shaved ice with fresh mango or a bowl of tofu and tapioca in a re-creation of a street in 1970s Kaohsiung City, down to the lanterns, brick walls and wooden benches. The restaurant is aptly named Memory Corner.

From his spot in the parking lot, right by the entrance to the food court, the four-faced Buddha is still looking over the Golden Village. Since they put him here, he's watched as people have made a life in this city. Thirty years later, they're still coming. As the skies roar overhead, he watches as the planes from Air China and Cathay Pacific touch down at the airport with the latest arrivals.

QUICK FACTS ABOUT RICHMOND

- The city was established November 10, 1879—seven years before Vancouver incorporated.
- Richmond has the largest Chinese diaspora population in North America.
- Richmond is home to Steveston—today, Canada's largest small-craft harbour. At the turn of the twentieth century, it bustled with canneries, shops, farms and homes. But it faced declines during the Depression and again during World War II, when its Japanese community was interned under the War Measures Act.

PENDER HARBOUR

A Beachcomber's Love Story

ABI HAYWARD

(2019)

WHEN I REACH Anne Clemence on the phone, her accent is unmistakeably English and she speaks with a smile in her voice. I've called her because I am collecting stories about the heyday of log salvaging in British Columbia.

Log salvagers also go by the name of beachcombers, or log salvors. They scour the waters and beaches for loose logs, most of which have escaped while being towed from point to point, and sell them to brokers who resell them to be milled.

Decades ago, log salvaging provided enough money and adventure to attract Anne Clemence and many others, even spawning a hit CBC television show, *The Beachcombers*. Though scarcer today, log salvagers still ply B.C.'s coast. Some forty scavenge along the Fraser River, one expert told me. But the best days are over, I keep hearing.

I ask Anne, who is eighty-six when we speak, when she first started log salvaging.

"Oh, when I met Sam Lamont!" she says instantly.

Anne had moved to Canada from England in 1960. After training as a nurse in London, she and a friend moved to Ottawa, road-tripped through the States, and found themselves living in North Vancouver. Anne heard about a nursing position in Pender Harbour and took it.

There she met Sam, a sturdy man sixteen years her senior, with a crewcut and a Celtic look to him.

"He used to bring the nurses oysters or fish or whatever he had," Anne remembers. "I'd heard about this guy that came in to see the girls. But he was such a nice kind. You never had any trouble with him! He used to take anybody that was off-duty out for a boat ride. So that appealed to me."

Before long, Anne was going out on the boat with Sam regularly. When the hospital that employed Anne closed, she moved in with Sam and they started working together. He was already salvaging logs.

Their boat was called *Vulture*.

"The log salvors were always hanging around the back of the tugboats when they were towing logs. You know, hovering. Waiting for logs to come out," explains Anne. "And sometimes the skipper would call on the radio, and say 'The vultures are behind me!'"

Sam decided to claim the nickname. Anne laughs. "It was free advertising, because if they ever said that the vultures were here, it was us."

It was very exciting, Anne says. "We never knew when we were going to go out. We didn't have regular hours. We had to be ready to drop everything we were doing, just to grab some food. And away you went. It was a very higgledy-piggledy sort of a life, I suppose."

And not one likely to make you rich. Anne says she and Sam didn't clear $20,000 in a year. They had to make compromises.

A friend once asked Anne if she missed the culture back in England. She thought about it. "At one point, we'd almost seen every single play that was on in London," she says. But go back? No. Who wants to see another play "with all this country around you with all the wild stuff?"

When Anne and Sam met, Sam already had two sons. She was not the mothering sort, she says, and didn't want to have kids of her own. "Where are you going to put a toddler on a boat pulling logs?" she asks.

Working on the log salvage boat could be dangerous, especially given that bad weather was when salvagers made money. Storms caused the logs towed by tugboats to come free and scatter into the sea.

"I mean, we didn't pray for bad weather," Anne laughs. "But we knew when the bad weather hit, we'd have work—and you weren't paid unless you turned in the logs."

Sam and Anne had built their own house next to the ocean in Garden Bay and had it organized such that they could drop everything in a second and head down to the boat. They placed radios throughout the house so that they could listen for a turn in the weather—or some captain's luck.

Sweet words to hear over the airwaves were "something

like 'We're losing logs!' Or 'Oh, we've had to drop it,'" explains Anne. "That was from the skipper who was in a bad spot and he had to drop his whole tow to get the boat back into shelter."

Then Anne and Sam would be out on the ocean.

They had some close calls working those big spills. Anne recalls one time she and Sam were on Vancouver's English Bay.

There had been a large spill of "massive cedars," Anne says, and a swell had taken the logs up the beach and mounded gravel and stones against them.

Anne knew it would take a lot of power to free the logs and drag them down the beach and into the sea. Anne kept the boat in place while Sam rowed ashore and jumped down into the sand. He wrapped a chain around a log and hooked it up to the towline connected to the boat. Theoretically, when the chain was pulled, it would twist and free the log.

"So he did this and I gave it a pull, a *good* pull, and nothing happened," says Anne. "So I thought, 'Oh my golly, ought to give it a bit more than that.'"

Anne backed up the boat, letting out some towline to give it some slack. It was important to have the boat lined up with the towline. "If it pulled off to one side, you'd capsize... So you had to be careful."

"So I had everything lined up and I gave it the works."

Suddenly, the tension ruptured one of the links at the end of the towline, and the line recoiled, hitting Anne down her left side.

The next thing she knew, she was sitting in the deck bucket against the back wall of the boat's cabin. She was bleeding from the head.

"Sam, poor Sam, came back looking as if he'd seen a ghost," Anne remembers. But as she came round, sitting in the bucket, she felt strangely comfortable. She laughs at the memory. "I thought, 'I don't know why I haven't tried sitting here before!'"

Anne was lucky. She and Sam had been working with other boats on that log spill, and an ambulance had been called. The other salvagers had seen what had happened; they made sure Anne and Sam got back to the dock. Anne was in hospital for a week with the cut on her head and a few cracked ribs. Her bruises blossomed in the perfect impression of braided rope.

While recuperating, she worried about Sam, now on his own chasing logs. "If you're out working like that by yourself, it's pretty dangerous," Anne says.

For a week more, she was on worker's compensation pay. Then she couldn't take it any longer. She showed up at the dock to join Sam aboard *Vulture*. "I couldn't do much, but at least I was with Sam," she says.

Anne and Sam gave up beachcombing in 1978. She vividly remembers the decision. Sam had just gotten off the phone after talking to Gulf Sort and Salvage, the outfit that bought their logs. "They were going to cut our price, or something or other that made him mad," she says. "And he turned to me and he said, 'I think we should quit.'"

"I said, 'Sure.' And so we quit."

They were ready. There wasn't enough money in the game anymore because movers of logs were getting better at keeping them. Nowadays, logs are tied up in bundles to be transported, rather than floating loose between boomsticks.

"Another thing was the weather forecasting," Anne says. "They brought in satellite imaging and the forecasts were getting more and more accurate." This allowed the tugboats to plan for bad weather, which was when the big spills tended to happen.

"It was the end of an era," she sighs. She and Sam sold *Vulture*. Then Sam fixed up a big sailboat, named *Kivak*, and the two of them explored the West Coast together for many years.

One day in 1992, they were tied up in a small, remote bay on Princess Royal Island, where they had spent many happy summers. Sam felt a pain in his chest and gradually went unconscious. He'd had a heart attack a few years before.

"I tried CPR and everything," Anne says.

After trying to get on the radio to the air-sea rescue, Anne finally got through to Prince Rupert. They sent a boat down, she says, but by the time they arrived, Sam was dead.

"They were very, very good and very helpful and they took his body away. And then I came back on the boat with Sam's son."

Anne pauses. "We find that we can live through things. I mean, the alternative isn't very good."

Among those who came down from Port Clements for Sam Lamont's funeral was an old log-salvaging friend named Dave Unsworth. Dave told me that Sam was one of the best beachcombers he had known. When I asked him what makes a good beachcomber, he said that it was about being a decent human being.

"And you need to be stubborn to put up with the environment. Sam was really good."

When I reached her, Anne was still living in the house she and Sam built by the sea in Garden Bay. It's where she answered my phone call.

Long ago, she stopped sailing on *Kivak*. But she waited for a long while before she sold it. She says it felt like giving a part of Sam away.

Anne has arthritis, a new hip replacement, and a rowboat beached in front of her home. After she heals from her hip operation, she plans to row out onto the water and, as best she can, return to "poking around the coast"—the joy that she and Sam shared.

It is B.C.'s ragged edge that "I always loved," Anne says. "I mean, that's why I came. And stayed."

QUICK FACTS ABOUT PENDER HARBOUR

→ Pender Harbour was the winter village site of the shíshálh Nation. It was at this site the community hosted coming-of-age rituals, spiritual ceremonies and potlatches that lasted weeks or months.

→ Officially, an Englishman named Charlie Irvine is said to be the first non-Indigenous person to settle in the area. But other sources suggest that the first non-Indigenous resident was actually a Chinese man who began a fish saltery.

→ Among settlers, Pender Harbour developed a reputation as a difficult land to cultivate, and a difficult place to make a living. It became known as Hardscratch.

LASQUETI ISLAND

A Wild and Woolly Issue

ANDREA BENNETT

(2021)

ON LASQUETI ISLAND, you're either a pro-sheeper or an anti-sheeper.

In mid-August, after speaking with over a dozen Lasquetians—and spotting several small herds of feral sheep from a distance—I find myself on the north end of the island feeding Rosemary, a previously feral sheep, a mix of grains from the palm of my hand.

It's hot and smoky, and the tide is high in nearby Mud Bay. If I move too quickly, Rosemary shuffles backwards in the dry grass, her midsection hefting from side to side. This skittishness is understandable: marine biologist Anna Smith rescued Rosemary earlier this year after she was abandoned by her mother, one of the island's feral sheep, at three days old.

In April, after rescuing Rosemary, Smith received a call about another ewe on the south end of the island who'd been shot with a crossbow. The bolt was still embedded in the sheep, which had recently given birth. Its lamb was small, weighing just four pounds, and it had no wool.

Smith extracted the bolt and rehabbed the ewe, whom she named Thyme. The lamb, Sage, seemed to thrive for a few months, before dying of what Smith suspects was a selenium deficiency resulting from being born prematurely.

Depending on who you talk to, the feral sheep population is either the gem of Lasqueti Island or a problem to be solved. Or perhaps that's oversimplifying it.

Many islanders harbour both an affinity for the sheep and a desire to ensure that their "herbivory"—consumption of both wild and cultivated plants and grasses—doesn't have too deleterious an impact on local wildflowers, food gardens and the forest's understory.

But this year, as the island updates its official community plan, the sheep are a lightning rod for controversy.

The pro-sheepers, as they refer to themselves, would prefer to maintain the existing objective included in the plan: "to preserve and support balanced control of the local feral/heritage sheep which are a valued part of the community and its history."

Their opposition—colloquially referred to, maybe unfairly, as "anti-sheepers"—have argued that this wording needs to be updated to reflect that "heritage" has specific, defined meanings and that preserving the sheep as is may mean sacrificing other flora and fauna.

In January 2020, after twenty-seven meetings and seven public forums, the island's Official Community Plan Review Steering Committee made a series of recommendations for updates. Among them was to edit the existing wording about sheep, so that it referred to them as an "exotic species" rather than a "feral/heritage" one, and to "minimize the impacts of invasive exotic species on native fauna and flora."

For some anti-sheepers, this language offered a useful compromise. But to most of the pro-sheepers, it registered as a threat.

Functionally, the wording change would not have altered much. The island comprises mostly private land, and residents are free to do more or less as they wish with sheep that wander onto their property. Symbolically, though, pro-sheepers felt the change would be the beginning of a slippery slope that could lead to more fences, less fondness and, ultimately, fewer and fewer sheep.

THE FIRST SHEEP probably arrived on Lasqueti, a small island nestled in the Strait of Georgia, in the late 1800s. According to Elda Copley Mason's book *Lasqueti Island: History and Memory*, Albion George Tranfield arrived with sheep in tow in the early 1860s. Tranfield, Mason writes, "made regular trips to dispose of the mutton in his Nanaimo meat markets."

A land surveyor visited in 1875 and found two settlers on the island—Tranfield, and another man named Captain Pearse. Each man owned about two hundred sheep each.

Pro-sheepers tend to believe that today's feral sheep are related to these sheep. An unsubstantiated rumour contends they arrived with the first Spanish explorers, those who renamed the island Lasqueti in the late eighteenth century. Others believe they were let loose later, maybe in the 1930s.

Another point of disagreement relates to how many feral sheep live on the island—anywhere from three hundred to a thousand, according to the Lasquetians I interviewed.

In February 2015, teachers, students and volunteers from False Bay School on the island did a sheep count. Andrew Fall, a qathet regional director who's also an adjunct professor in the School of Resource and Environmental Management at Simon Fraser University, helped design the study. It wasn't a proper survey, Fall says, but it allowed them to come up with a low estimate of 259 adults and eighty-one lambs.

Fall keeps his own sheep: a rare heritage breed called Soay, originally from the St. Kilda archipelago in Scotland. (His work to preserve this breed colours his perception about whether Lasqueti's feral sheep should be called "heritage," as it's impossible to know if they are a heritage breed without doing a full DNA analysis.)

Fall estimates Lasqueti to be home to about four hundred feral sheep. This means that the island, with just under four hundred year-round residents, is home to more sheep than humans on any given rainy November day.

"Have you ever watched lambs?" Tom Weinerth, a pro-sheeper who moved to Lasqueti in 1970, asks me over the phone. "I call it popcorn. All of a sudden, one of them will just pop into the air, and then all the other ones around, they'll just start popping up. They're so happy to be alive."

In the winter, Weinerth supplements the sheep's diets with grain. This past winter, he and a neighbour nursed a sheep who'd injured her leg. He enjoys seeing them gambolling by on his property.

Weinerth, a spokesperson for a pro-sheep delegation to a Local Trust Committee meeting in April, says if people want to move to an island with lush flora left ungrazed, they should choose another island. Why move to one with sheep if you don't like sheep?

LASQUETI, WHICH IS LOCATED in the traditional territories of the Tla'amin Nation, as well as several other Coast Salish nations, might be the gulfiest of the Gulf Islands. It is, as the CBC puts it, a "counter-culture enclave."

Or, as one accurate if overly bewildered Global News documentary begins: "Imagine an island so secluded there's no power, no paved roads and no plumbing in most cases either."

Residents of the island, many of whom arrived in the 1970s (or who have come looking for what settlers were seeking in the 1970s), have worked to ensure that the island's ferry is passenger-only, that the roads remain gravel and that land can't be subdivided smaller than ten acres.

To the Global filmmakers, these rules enshrine a hippieish, throwback style of life. And maybe they do, in part. But they also exist, as someone ventured at a recent Local Trust Committee meeting, to keep away "rich people"—people who might turn up their noses at outhouses and a lack of steady electricity. A recent community survey found that around forty-five percent of respondents from Lasqueti, compared with twenty percent from the region as a whole, had household incomes between $10,000 and $29,999 per year.

These modest means point to feral flocks having added value—something the suggested wording for the new community plan recognizes, saying the "exotic species... may have value to the community as a source of local food."

Gail Fleming, who moved to Lasqueti forty-two years ago, chose the island in part because food sources were plentiful.

"There was salmon, there was rockfish, clams, oysters, wild berries, mushrooms, abandoned orchards and sheep—and even free-range cows at one point," she says. Much has changed. The Salish Sea is becoming too acidic for oysters, salmon are endangered, and many of the orchards she used to access have been abandoned or taken over by people who have not kept them up. But the sheep are still there.

"Seldom a long period of time goes by somebody doesn't show up at the door and say, 'I got a sheep today,' and hands me a package of lamb," Fleming says.

And she cares more about food security than the wildflowers the sheep are eating. "I've never been to a wildflower barbecue," she says.

Wendy Schneible, vice-president of the Lasqueti Island Nature Conservancy, has been on the island for forty-seven years. She arrived in her twenties as a back-to-the-lander who first lived in a teepee.

Schneible, who disagrees with calling the sheep "heritage," is okay with the other aspects of the old community plan wording that calls for "balanced control" of the sheep population—the way things are handled currently doesn't actually control the sheep, or balance their needs with those of native plants and trees, however, and the status quo needs to change.

"There is no 'balance,'" she says. "There is no 'control.' They want to maintain the status quo, which isn't what the actual wording says."

At the John Osland Nature Reserve, which covers about sixty acres, Schneible shows me two fenced "exclosures" LINC has set up to keep feral sheep (and native deer) out. Outside the fences, sheep and deer paths crisscross the mossy, rocky outcrops. The bottom branches of the cedars have been stripped of greenery, and some daring sheep or deer have even taken nibbles of stinging nettles and thistles.

Inside the four-year-old exclosures, which abut a marsh, the grass is longer and the plants more abundant and varied. The goal of the exclosures is to track the impacts of herbivory and the process of recovery and restoration.

LINC has no official mandate about the sheep, Schneible tells me later, and the organization has no desire to either eliminate or take responsibility for them. Her opinion about the community plan wording is merely hers as an individual.

Osland's circumstances are mirrored on the south end of the island, where Ken Lertzman and Dana Lepofsky live. Lertzman, a member of LINC and a professor emeritus of forest ecology and management at Simon Fraser University, and Lepofsky, a professor of archaeology at SFU, have both written letters in support of changing the community plan's wording around sheep.

They've fenced off a small part of the property they've shared with several other families since 1989. Outside the fence, the property has been denuded of most greenery other than moss. Even the swordfern, which Lertzman describes as "not good eating," has been chewed to its base.

Inside the fence, Lertzman points out plants that have regained their footing after being kept from sheep and deer: starflower, salal, huckleberries, salmonberries, elderberries, maple trees and deer fern.

As a forest ecologist, Lertzman's educated guess is that tree species such as western red cedar have not regenerated effectively after land clearing on some parts of the island, in part because of artificially high levels of "browsing"—in other words, because sheep and deer have eaten young shoots and trees.

To really understand the impacts of sheep on the forests and the flora and fauna they support, Lertzman says, the island needs to gather solid data.

The exclosures LINC has created at Osland, and some new exclosures they have planned for the Mount Trematon Nature Reserve, will allow them to gather information about the impacts of herbivory. Other important data to gather could include DNA analyses of the sheep population, a more accurate sheep count, and a survey of their health.

Many people I spoke with who appreciated the sheep but were worried about their ecological impacts also tended to worry that the sheep probably had parasites, went hungry in the winter, and needed shearing. Gathering data could provide information about these issues.

Anna Smith, the biologist who took in Rosemary, Thyme and Sage, also thinks it's a good idea to properly assess the island's sheep population, their genetic variation and their herd ranges.

She agrees, too, with investigating the impact of grazing and browsing on the island's ecosystems, but she cautions that some differences people see on the north end of the island, where there are fewer sheep, and the south end of the island, where there are more sheep, may be due to differences in micro-climates rather than simply being a result of their presence.

Most pro-sheepers also wouldn't mind gathering data about the sheep's numbers, their ranges and their genetics. In fact, many believe that DNA testing could support the idea that Lasqueti's sheep—which are not susceptible, for example, to scrapie, a fatal disease similar to mad cow—are a hardy, heritage sort of stock. The sheep wouldn't have survived a century on the island if they were not relatively well and thriving, pro-sheepers say.

But they don't necessarily trust LINC—a group that contains members many of them perceive as "anti-sheep"—to facilitate research.

When I first stumbled across Lasqueti's feral sheep, I'd wondered why I, like many settlers, found something about them inherently fascinating. I'd set my assumptions aside when I found out about lamb barbecues—but revisiting the question, the fact the sheep are a food source doesn't cover all the bases.

For a lot of pro-sheep Lasquetians, it might be something about their previous domestication that provides a draw. Maybe, much like the aims and goals of the back-to-the-land movement, the sheep used to lead penned-in, circumscribed lives and now are free.

(My hunch about Tom Weinerth is different. Though he's eaten lamb barbecue in the past, he's now a vegetarian, and I get the sense from talking to him that the sheep are his treasured friends.)

"It is in many ways much more of a social issue than a biological issue," Lertzman says, mulling over why the issue of sheep animates the community, even dividing it. "The biological aspect is straightforward, but the social aspect of it is much more complex."

To Lepofsky, assigning feral sheep "heritage" status is a problem tied to colonial assumptions. "I have a deeper interest in longer-term heritage and connections to place," she says. "When I think of heritage, I think instead about Indigenous heritage and that of the heritage ecosystems that Indigenous peoples were and are a part of."

DURING THAT MID-AUGUST heat wave, Lasqueti's trustees, the chair of the Islands Trust Council, some Islands Trust staff, Andrew Fall and about twelve community members met outside Lasqueti Island's Judith Fisher Centre. It was time to hash out whether to change the community plan language for feral sheep from "heritage" to "exotic" species.

The previous day, a LINC member had told me they expected that most of the people in attendance would be pro-sheepers. As the meeting progressed, it became clear they'd guessed right.

The meeting, which became a bit heated, led to what, if you like dad jokes, you could call a "ewe-turn."

During the discussion, some termed the process Orwellian (both 1984 and *Animal Farm* were referenced), there was heckling, and there was someone calling, "hear! hear!" after another person said the sheep were important to food security and he'd been eating them for seventy years. In the end, the council voted to let the sheep remain "heritage" sheep, a "valued part of the community and its history."

The community members in attendance seemed relieved. As the meeting ended, Weinerth, who'd been one of the more vocal attendees, chatted happily with other community members. "There's still some touching up to do," he told me later, on the phone. "But I'm satisfied."

Smith believes the trustees made the right decision. "It's a good thing," she said. "It's really about the perception."

The day after the meeting, I bike to Fall's farm. As we feed the female Soay sheep a mix of a little grain pellets, which they like, and barley, which they dislike, I recall a conversation I had with Fall before I came to the island.

The feral sheep, he told me, come under the jurisdiction of the province, so any policy contained in the community plan about them will be an advocacy policy—in other words, like Smith noted, a policy that affects perception, rather than one that comes with any power to enforce anything.

Regardless of what happens with the community plan, Fall says, people will still be able to harvest the sheep for food or take them in to provide care if they get sick or injured.

And though the wording feels important to many islanders, the underlying dispute has yet to be resolved.

Only an interest-based community process—where Lasquetians could come together to share their values and concerns—has any chance of resolving this issue, Fall tells me.

"The fabric that holds a community together is more easily torn than woven," he says.

QUICK FACTS ABOUT LASQUETI ISLAND

→ Lasqueti Island was home to the Pentlatch Band and is in the traditional territories of the Homalco, Tla'amin and Klahoose Nations.

→ Indigenous artifacts have been found dating back thousands of years. Of these, the most unique is possibly the midden: ancient mounds of discarded shellfish shells found on the island's many beaches.

→ No cars are permitted on the passenger ferry to Lasqueti Island, and all roads on the island are unpaved. The island is not connected to BC Hydro's electrical power grid.

SATURNA ISLAND

The Worst Windstorm in BC Hydro's History

SOFIA OSBORNE

(2019)

I WAKE EARLY. The walls are shaking. It sounds like the rest of the house has melted away, like my room is a ship in a storm. How can the wind be so loud? How can it rush through the walls like a sieve? I run down the stairs in the chill.

My dad's in the living room, his weathered face staring out the window at the sea. He chose this house on the east tip of Saturna Island for the seclusion and the view: the ocean and the San Juan Islands, the rocky cliff.

Together we watch the waves, so choppy they're stark white, tangle on the rocks. Mariners would call this a force 10. Later, I find out today marks the worst windstorm in BC Hydro's history. To me, it's the day I realize I could be blown off my feet.

My dad points to my cup on the table, the water inside it rippling. "The house is shaking," he says. "I've never seen anything like this."

"Are you worried?" I ask.

"No," he replies quickly. "It's stood through so many storms."

Here's what we don't yet know: the wind is blowing over a hundred kilometres an hour, swirling to hit us from three directions. It won't stop for eight hours. The Gulf Islands will be the hardest hit. The shifting winds, high

speeds and four hundred millimetres of rain that fell over the last few weeks has created the perfect stew of conditions to uproot even healthy trees.

By the afternoon the power is out. The inverter for the backup battery isn't working and we're not sure why. My dad's solar panels are still hooked up to the grid, so they're no use to us now. We have no internet, no phone, no cell service. We are as far away from the ferry terminal as possible, as my dad preferred. He's only lived here four years; he's seen storms before, but they weren't like this.

We're supposed to leave the island to go to Vancouver for Christmas and have a reservation on the 4:30 ferry. Is it running? We have no idea. But we have nothing better to do than drive over to the terminal with our suitcases, just in case.

While we pack, my dad says, "You know, I really admire how calm you're being about all this. It's very grown-up."

"There's no use panicking," I say, carefully filling my water bottle only halfway—we're rationing what remains of the water pressure.

As soon as I get outside, I'm shoved off balance, nearly knocked to the ground. The sky is blue, beautiful, but the trees are sideways. I look at my dad but we don't say anything. As we roll out of the driveway, we see Cliffside Road; the pavement is a lawn of evergreen needles. A minefield of branches and downed power lines. The car crunches over them. "Don't worry," my dad says hesitantly. "There's no power." It's a calculated risk. I close my eyes, hold my breath before the tires make contact.

This is the only road to the rest of the island, the ferry terminal, civilization. It's so narrow that what should be one lane is split in two, snaking between a cliff and the ocean. We drive on like this, my dad's hands at ten and two, knuckles white. My eyes are on the lines on his forehead, the way he squints in focus, then on the treetops above us that pitch back and forth.

My dad calls this road "The Cathedral" for the way the arbutuses arch over the pavement. Usually, when we pass under them, I feel transported to a world where life moves slower and there's nothing more important than the beauty of this island. Where the stress of life in Vancouver is cleansed to nothing. That's the feeling my dad was chasing when he moved here after he retired from law and teaching. The life he wanted when he put up his solar panels and bought his electric car. That's the life I want too, a lot of the time.

Now the cathedral is closing in on us. The trees lie in pieces on the road, jutting out like javelins.

We're getting close to the main route that will take us the length of Saturna, East Point Road. The sky is fading and the trees are no longer trees, just black ghosts. As we lose the light, I lose any hope of getting off the island.

How could the ferries be running? How had we ever thought they might be? It's then that we reach the final obstacle: a tree lying definitively across the road, blocking our path. My dad swears. "There's no way the ferry is running anyway," I say quietly.

"Well, we can't get to it now." He turns the car around.

On the way back, I notice every toppled tree that wasn't there before. They're everywhere. The car, which had felt safe, is now a slowly moving target. The wind catches up to us and we get blocked again; another tree hovering too low over the pavement. We're fenced in.

"Now what?" My question hangs limp, quickly blown away.

My dad stares at the downed tree like he can lift it back up with the strength of his convictions. He opens the car door, gets out, pulls at the tree branches to try to break them, to create a tiny hole we can slither through, but they barely bend. I watch his body twist with the effort and I think of his back, how he threw it out just a month ago, how sore he'll be tomorrow.

"Come on," I call out to him. "We won't fit anyway. Can we find someone with a chainsaw?"

We do: John, whose family has lived on the island for so long there's a road named after them, and Karen, a carpenter and cabinetmaker who installed my dad's new floors, are out roaming the roads in their trucks. They're taking the downed trees apart meticulously—mid-storm—and marking them with fluorescent orange tape. Karen lives out our way; she'll take us back, my dad says. We meet more trees along the road, and as my dad and Karen cut through the thick trunks and pull at the pieces, I sit frozen in the passenger seat, feeling trapped.

When we're a few houses away from home, Karen peels off down her road and my dad starts talking about how lucky we are. The adrenaline is radiating off him, but all I feel is wary. We're by our neighbour's house, close to home but chainsaw-less, when we see the biggest trees of all blocking our way.

"We can leave the car here," my dad says slowly, "grab the suitcases and crawl under the trees. It's not a long walk."

God, no, I think.

A pair of headlights appears through the gaps in the tree trunks.

"Let me see who it is," my dad says.

When he leaves the car, I lose it. It starts with hyperventilation, then breathless sobs. The forest is so tall on both sides of me and the roots that I thought were so sturdy now seem so fragile. They could give way and a tree could just crush me, and all I would see, if I saw anything, would be the trunk racing toward me. If I was lucky I'd die instantly, but it's just as likely a branch would puncture me and I would bleed out, waiting for medical attention—how would a helicopter even be able to fly in this storm? They'd never get me to the hospital; I'd die a slow death. I'm choking on my sobs by the time my dad comes back to the car.

He's excited. It's Jeremiah and his chainsaw. Then he sees my face. "Oh, oh no, sweetie." He looks down at me. "It's okay, it's okay, we're almost home." He closes the door to go help, leaving me alone to fill the car with panicked tears.

It feels like both seconds and years until Jeremiah finishes hauling away the blockade. I watch him work and I think about how he's just a year or two older than me, but he's coming alive while I'm shrinking. As we pass him—he's going off to find more trees to conquer—my dad rolls down the passenger window to say thank you again, and I hide my tear-streaked face in my jacket sleeve. When we get home, I lie on the couch in my parka, hood up. I can't say anything as my dad apologizes to me. "It's okay that you felt scared. It's completely understandable."

We get off the island the next day. There's a four-sailing wait at Swartz Bay, even with the extra boats. My dad won't go back to Saturna until after New Year's; his power will be out for eight days; his leftovers will go rancid in the freezer. His phone won't come back online until mid-January.

In Vancouver I watched the news roll in: boats broke loose in White Rock, crashing through the pier and leaving a man stranded on the other side. The generator for Nanaimo's water plant failed, putting it out of commission for twelve hours. I thought about all the stories I'll never hear: each of the 756,000 people who lost power, who had to change their Christmas plans, who had trees puncture their roofs or crush their cars, who realized how little they could control. Did they feel as small as I did in the face of the storm?

Most of them got their power back in the first twenty-four hours. But there were people in remote areas, like my dad and me, who took days and days to reach. In some places, BC Hydro had to send helicopters out to survey the damage because the roads were impassable.

Almost two thousand spans of wire came down in the storm—five hundred on Salt Spring alone. Hydro had to deal with 5,800 trouble calls; an average storm sees three hundred.

It was the "storm of the century, one for the history books"—except it won't be.

The climate is changing. While storm frequency is hard to project, the number of storms BC Hydro has responded to has tripled in the last five years, and the number of customer outages during major storms has increased alongside at a similar pace.

My dad has a chainsaw now, tucked in the back of his trunk. I get scared when I think of him using it, at seventy years old, out in the wind and the sideways rain, hacking away. But he is a superhero, and of course he would want to help his community.

When I think about my dad on Saturna, I think about how untenable his situation could get as the storms get worse and worse, and he gets older. He thinks about this too, but he's doubled down. He loves this place; it's home. If he could go back and change his mind, he wouldn't, he told me. I know my dad; he takes risks for the things he loves. That scares me too.

My dad will be more prepared next time. He'll have a backup to his backup system, enough food and water to last for weeks, and, of course, the chainsaw. Maybe he'll work toward going completely off the grid—in case of apocalypse. And I'll worry every time I call him and get the busy signal of a dead phone.

QUICK FACTS ABOUT SATURNA ISLAND

→ Saturna gets less rain than either Victoria or Vancouver. This is because it is located in the shadow of the Vancouver Island mountains, which draw moisture from incoming storms.

→ The island is named after the Spanish schooner *Santa Saturnina,* which made contact in 1791.

→ The island is thirty-one square kilometres and has a year-round population of approximately three hundred people. It has no banks, pharmacies or full-time doctors.

THETIS LAKE PARK

How I Salvaged My Sense of Wonder

TIM B. ROGERS

(2022)

IN THESE HARD TIMES for the planet, I verged on despair. Then one day in the forest changed everything.

Some time ago I was standing beside a drab cement sluice that rerouted what used to be a small creek around a shopping mall in the British Columbia town of Cranbrook. Bill Westover, the region's long-standing fisheries biologist, was with me. He recalled how he had once fished for cutthroat trout in this used-to-be stream. "Big ones, too," he sighed. "Just a little bit at a time, this place got carved up, and before we knew what happened, it was gone. Then we forgot there'd ever been a creek here."

He looked at the sluice and then into the distance. "Death by a thousand small cuts," he mused. "And there doesn't seem to be a lot we can do about it—not enough Band-Aids."

Now, over thirty years later, I find myself inundated with stories about these thousand cuts—perhaps now multiplied to tens of thousands, millions. They're everywhere, converging on a tipping point where the world we've come to know is in peril. I am trying to resist being gripped by a kind of enviro-paralysis. It's depressing. Maybe Bill was right.

But every now and then this story gets flipped on its head. Something pokes through the gloom and changes things. Maybe it's the return of salmon to the Elwha River after the removal of a couple of dams. Or the repatriation of wild bison to Canadian mountain parks. Or wolves to Yellowstone.

Whenever such stories come my way, I find myself reliving that sluice-side discussion with Bill.

I wish I'd known enough back then to say, "Yeah, Bill, but maybe healing by a million wee steps is something worth thinking about. Perhaps that's a better mantra... At least we'd be doing something."

But where to start?

For me, in my seventies, it began with walks in the woods that opened in me a part of my mind, my soul, long stowed away and forgotten. That part of us we call our imagination. Our sense of wonder at possibilities sensed but unseen.

Why had it taken so long for me to rediscover this part of me, and what had locked it away?

I'M A RETIRED SOCIAL SCIENTIST. A lifetime ago, I cut my scientific teeth in experimental psychology. This research discipline has always worked incredibly hard to convince itself, and others, that it is a science. A big part of its pitch involves an unflinching commitment to objectivity—to banish all signs of the ghost from the machine; to revel in unbiased knowledge; not to get too involved with the subject matter.

This was ingrained into me as a graduate student. I vividly remember the red ink that decorated the first draft of my thesis proposal, telling me to get rid of myself in the presentation and just talk data.

Later, as a professor, I became the one imposing this sterile message on graduate students preparing to be scientists.

Today, I recognize that this constant adherence to the language of "objectivity" had an enduring effect on me. It loomed large in my work, in my home life and in my view of the world in general. I became reluctant to let my imagination go—I learned to keep it under wraps. And as a result of such neglect, like many aspects of our natural environment, my internal landscape was scarred.

This all began to change when I ceased being a scientific professional, moved to Vancouver Island and eventually found the time to take daily, long walks in the woodlands surrounding Victoria. One of my favourite haunts became Thetis Lake Regional Park.

I remember like it was yesterday. Early June, after a dull, wet spring that felt like it would never end. A heavy mist hung just above the fir trees, reminding me of what had seemed like interminable months of rain and overcast skies. While the leaves had arrived, albeit reluctantly, there was this sense that nature had stalled. Nothing seemed to be on the move—we were stuck in a rut that prevented summer from making its presence felt. The air was harsh on my face as I moved into the trees.

My mood mirrored the featureless and seemingly suspended world around me. I trudged into the woods more out of habit than any intense desire to be there.

But then everything changed.

Coming around a curve in the trail, I encountered an old tree smattered with white shapes curling their way seductively up the trunk. They sketched alluring lines upwards, immediately catching my eye. I stopped in my tracks. Totally unexpected, these intricate forms punched a hole in my gloom.

My mood lightened to see such exuberant life. I smiled, probably laughed out loud, as I finally recognized this delightful growth of mushrooms artistically decorating the tree. I ran home to get my camera.

Excitement welled up as I set up my tripod—such unanticipated beauty, such a wonder of nature. I revelled in how each of the individual shelves that made up the larger shapes was, itself, a work of art—a soft white edge, seeming to wander at random, framing an incredible array of parallel forms, gills, that generated a vibrant sense of design and movement.

Their glorious abundance was stunning. The intricate designs of the gills framed a vision of "nature the great artist," casting lines and shapes in what could only be thought of as systematic randomness, like a priceless etching. What a masterpiece!

MY WOODS WALKS CHANGED. Now I walked in eager anticipation of another spectacle around the next corner.

I challenged myself to come to know some of the subtleties of the amazing ecosystems of the Pacific Northwest rainforest—particularly the hidden fungal life that spawned these beauties. Little did I know that I was on the cusp of an amazing voyage of reawakening, one that would have me tramping through the woods virtually every day of the year.

I began scouring whatever books I could find to try to understand some of the secrets underlying these amazing fungi. I was on what they call a "quiet hunt," searching for mushrooms—not to fill up a basket for the dining table, but to fill up my mind with whatever shapes, designs and knowledge nature was willing to make available.

Soon, however, I encountered a perplexing problem. These life forms do their best to keep themselves hidden from us humans. While occasionally fungi do show off as mushrooms, the vast majority of the time they live where we can't see them—underground or perhaps inside dead trees. Not only that, the vegetative fibres that make up these underground mycelia are quite fine, almost microscopic, so even if I wanted to dig them up, they'd still be hard to see.

Because fungi are so reluctant to show themselves, it's easy to get fooled into thinking they aren't particularly abundant or that important. But we'd be wrong.

Conservative estimates indicate there are somewhere between 2.2 and 3.8 million species of fungi on Earth, dwarfing the plant and animal kingdoms in terms of diversity. Their underground world is huge. For example, it's estimated that between one-fifth and one-tenth of the biomass in the soil of a Douglas fir forest, like the one I walk every day, is made up of fungal mycelia. That's a lot of hair-thin fibres.

The largest living organism on the planet, the "humongous fungus," lives not far south of here in the Malheur National Forest of eastern Oregon. It's estimated to cover 965 hectares, weigh somewhere between 6,800 and 32,000 tonnes, and be somewhere in the vicinity of 2,400 years old.

The functioning of our world depends on the decomposing capacities of some fungi. And the emerging view of the forest as a networked community is founded on the presence of fungi that enter into symbiotic relationships with all kinds of plants and trees.

And so fungi are the physical instantiation of the idea of ecological connectivity. Without a doubt, they are immensely important to sustaining life.

But they are largely invisible, and that turned out to be quite a challenge. How could I honour and more deeply appreciate the importance of these organisms if I couldn't see them and make them concrete and observable? How could I know them better without directly experiencing their presence?

As I tromped about in the local woods, I began to conjure imaginary pictures of the fungal mycelium in my mind. I visualized the complex network of thread-like fibres running beneath the ground, a vast web infiltrating the many fallen logs I was passing.

Sometimes, in my dreaming mind, I'd get the feeling I was walking over a gossamer bridge—the trail being the bridge's deck, the mycelium being what's holding it up. These made-up images created a sense of contact with the elusive mycelium, changing it from the abstract, invisible entity I'd read about into an alive presence. This increased my passion and caring, dare I say love, not only for the fungi here but also for the wondrous woodlands that I'm fortunate enough to visit each day.

PLEASE DON'T READ this essay as a rejection of the scientific method or the importance of striving for a fact-based understanding of our existences. Much of what I have said about fungal mycelia is drawn, after all, from the hard-won findings of researchers.

No, my intent is to remind that science, at any level, must be infused with imagination. That taking the measure of our world is a creative, intuitive enterprise at its heart. And that we do no service to young scientists if we cause them to feel embarrassed about engaging in flights of fancy like my dreaming of the vast, intertwined realm living below my feet in a forest. A sense of wonder and emotional connection sustains the emergence of new and innovative research.

When we get our knees wet, our hands dirty, our senses full, we should not distrust that delivered jolt to our nervous systems. We should embrace it as a reminder that each of us carries within us internal landscapes, some much hidden, some quite blighted, waiting to be revitalized.

By looking within and embracing what is mysterious as well as what is plainly there, we can better see the glories of the natural world. And then we are better able to lend our energies to healing this Earth by a million wee steps.

QUICK FACTS ABOUT THETIS LAKE PARK

→ Established in 1958, Thetis Lake Regional Park was Canada's first nature sanctuary. It's home to forty kilometres of recreational trails and two lakes.

→ In 1972, two teenage boys claimed to see a monster emerge from the depths of Thetis Lake. It had "silvery skin, sharp claws and spikes on its head." The RCMP investigated, but found no evidence. Curiously, the description of the monster exactly matched the appearance of the terrifying Gill-man from the 1954 movie *Creature from the Black Lagoon*.

→ The park is named after a British navy frigate, HMS *Thetis*, which patrolled B.C. waters during the mid-1800s gold rush. In Greek mythology, Thetis is a sea nymph—the goddess of water and the mother of Achilles.

VICTORIA

More *Deadwood* Than *Downton Abbey*

TOM HAWTHORN

(2023)

O VICTORIA, YOU DOWAGER HOME to the newlywed and nearly dead, you faded beauty with hanging flower baskets to please the tourists, you Lotus Land of palm trees and lush gardens, you progenitor of coffee shops with artisanal doughnuts as sacraments, you purveyor of craft beers and distilled spirits infused with sustainably harvested winged kelp, wherefore do you exist? As a cute anglophile playground for visitors, or as a cosmopolitan intellectual and cultural capital for a modern province, leaning into a global future while acknowledging its Indigenous roots?

HARRY AND MEGHAN came to Vancouver Island for a respite from an intrusive press corps. It did not take long for their idyll to be interrupted. News of their stay generated a tsunami of media attention. Much of the global reportage carried a predictable theme for a prince who was great-great-great-great-grandson of the monarch after whom the city was named.

Victoria, readers and viewers were told in 2020, as they have been for more than a century, was a city "more British than the British." Tea rooms. Double-decker buses. The grand Empress Hotel. Craigdarroch Castle. Fish and chips.

When you read that stuff, you half expect the locals to speak in Cockney rhyming slang. An American customer at a downtown bookstore once loudly proclaimed her disappointment at checkout that none of the staff spoke in the accent she expected. Had any of us tried, we would have sounded like Dick Van Dyke in *Mary Poppins*.

Outsiders might be lured here to witness the Old Country in a lush corner of the New World, but the Englishness of Victoria is tourism hokum, the city tarting up to cosplay Old Blighty to better take money from the out-of-town yokels.

The most recent census two years ago showed fewer than half of Greater Victoria's population of four hundred thousand residents were born in British Columbia. About one in five were born outside Canada. For immigrants who arrived since 2016, more were from the Philippines (585), India (300) and the United States (255) than from the United Kingdom (185). Nearly as many came from Syria (180). The one in five Victorians who identify as members of a visible minority is a number that can be expected to grow in coming years.

So where did the Little Britain reputation come from? In a word, marketing. But first some history.

The southern tip of what we now call Vancouver Island has been for more than a millennium the home of the Lekwungen-speaking peoples and their ancestors, as it is today. On March 13, 1843, James Douglas, chief factor of the Hudson's Bay Company, anchored off Clover Point. The next day, he selected a site known by the residents as Camosack, meaning "rush of water," for what would become Fort Victoria. He would write a letter to a friend describing what he saw: "The place itself is a perfect 'Eden' in the midst of the dreary wilderness of the North." By 1854, some 230 Europeans, including children, lived at the fort, a centre of the company's fur trade and a place of subsistence farming.

The city's future was changed forever on a sleepy Sunday morning in 1858 when the sidewheel steamer *Commodore* arrived in the harbour from San Francisco with more than 450 prospectors eager to find their fortune in gold on the mainland. In a few weeks, some twenty thousand men arrived in the city. They were transient and they were thirsty, armed and lonely. Wooden saloons, dance halls and brothels sprung up overnight. Early Victoria was more *Deadwood* than *Downton Abbey*.

Accommodation was so limited that many of the prospectors lived in tents struck on empty lots. The gold rush also created the city's first land rush; lots once available for $25 were suddenly changing hands for $3,000.

Among those flocking to the colony were free Black people from California. Douglas, who served as governor of the colony, promised full civil rights and freedoms to Black people who settled in the colony.

These new arrivals faced discrimination in Victoria from whites, whether British citizens or fellow Americans. When Black men were rejected for service with fire crews, they got permission from Douglas to form the Victoria Pioneer Rifle Corps, also known as the African Rifles. They paraded along the waterfront when ships filled with American prospectors arrived, the sight of free and armed Black men intended to be a warning and a reminder to the arrivals that they were now in a land without slavery.

Early Victoria was a vibrant place of many nationalities and languages, including Lekwungen and Chinook, the pidgin trading language of the region. They joined workers from China and Hawai'i. The first private book published on Vancouver Island, *The Fraser Mines Vindicated*, by Alfred Waddington, reported, "Victoria was assailed by an indescribable array of Polish [J]ews, Italian fishermen, French cooks, jobbers, speculators of every kind, land agents, auctioneers, hangers on at auctions, bummers, bankrupts, and brokers of every description."

In the decades following the first gold rush, more buildings in the downtown core were made of brick. Though we now think of the Victorian era as one of excessive prudery, sex work was common in the city bearing her name. Sex workers and clients met in Trounce Alley, while a few upscale brothels were to be found around the downtown core. One of these was on the upper floors of Duck's Block at 1316 Broad Street, a three-storey commercial brick building owned by former provincial finance minister Simeon Duck, not one to turn down profit.

After San Francisco was destroyed by the earthquake in 1906, several madams and their workers followed the route of the gold-rush hopefuls by heading north to Victoria. Their arrival coincided with a crackdown on the trade by a reformist mayor, who pushed the high-end brothels into the city's red zone. An influx of immigration from Britain starting late in the previous century coincided with measures by the city's elite to repress vice and impose a stricter code of public morality.

The city was undergoing another of its periodic land booms when the outbreak of war in Europe in the summer of 1914 brought an end to building and speculation, as well as tourism.

After the end of war and during the recovery following the Spanish flu, the city embarked on a marketing campaign to promote tourism that was successful beyond imagination. A booklet titled "The Call of Victoria" was distributed through the province's agent general's office in London, England. A catchphrase in the booklet—"Follow the birds to Victoria"—came to be a slogan reproduced on folders, brochures, postcards, windshield stickers and even billboards. Other come-ons offered a secondary tease: the Capital City, the City of Gardens, "Less rain, more sunshine." Victoria was described as a city of industry, an evergreen playground, a fishing fantasia and a golfing mecca in all four seasons. A bold graphic of white seagulls on a dark blue background captured the promise of an island vacation for a city not reachable by road.

Tourists flocked to the city, and they keep on coming to this day. Greater Victoria will get about four million visitors this year, or ten for every inhabitant. Cherry and plum blossoms are a sign of spring, and so is the arrival of the first cruise ship. In 2023, it was the *Sapphire Princess*, on April 12, with another 319 docking visits to unload about 850,000 passengers before the season ends in October.

Businesses sought to cater to the out-of-towners, playing on clichés. For decades, you could visit a replica of Shakespeare's birthplace at the Olde English Inn. You could have mushy peas at the Old British Fish and Chip Shop. You could see Queen Victoria and Jack the Ripper alike rendered in paraffin at the Royal London Wax Museum. At King Arthur's Round Table Dining Lounge, the front door was opened by a Beefeater in red uniform, while the roast beef specialty was served on Royal Crown Derby china. You could tour the city aboard a Royal Blue Line Sightseeing bus.

Today, all are gone. The Olde English Inn is the site of a major townhome and condominium development. The wax museum has been closed for more than a decade, with the figures disassembled and the waxen heads and hands (the most vulnerable features) stored in the climate-controlled basement of the owner's home. The chippy, renamed the Old Vic, closed earlier this year after nine decades. Its location will be redeveloped as part of a new 135-room hotel centred on Duck's Block, the former home to high-end brothels.

The news of each of these closings was greeted in some corners as the coming of an apocalypse. Long-time residents of Victoria have many qualities. Resistance to change is one of the less appealing. They stand on guard for NIMBY-ville. Don't change a thing.

Top of the oppo list has been the closing of the Old

Town display at the Royal BC Museum, which includes scaled-down replica facades of the business district of a hypothetical, turn-of-the-century British Columbia town, and the proposal to replace the museum with a modern, seismically safe, Indigenous-centred, billion-dollar landmark. After all, why would Victoria want to build a Sydney Opera House–like landmark in a city dependent on tourism with tax dollars largely provided by people who don't live in the city? The museum plans have been shelved, and even Old Town might come back, a sop to the anxieties animated in some corners by acts of reconciliation. Don't get me started. Old Town was a tired and ahistorical nod to European supremacy. ("It will be the story of the white man's impact on British Columbia," reads the original brochure, "his technological successes, his cultural impacts...") It is so last century.

Those who would prefer to set Victoria in aspic will say do not tear down another tree, do not build another house, certainly do not add apartment blocks, extra suites, laneway houses or infill houses of any kind. Everything must be preserved to maintain a hint of an idyllic near-past before things started to go to hell.

A quarter-century ago, housing was plentiful in the capital. Low-rise apartment blocks lined Cook Street, offering affordable housing for students and seniors just a short walk from downtown.

Many of those blocks have since been purchased by real estate investment trusts, the tenants evicted, slipshod mass renovations completed (albeit with eye-catching stoves and refrigerators) and rents doubled or tripled. Airbnb and Vrbo suck up many more apartments. Some renovated historical buildings and even twelve-storey condo blocks are almost entirely rented to vacation travellers.

And that is ratcheting up pressures that give the lie to provincial capital as placid English garden. The baristas and bookstore clerks who help make living in the city so pleasurable an experience are left in a precarious state when they lose their homes. They take roommates or live in micro apartments no bigger than a parking stall, or are pushed ever farther into the suburbs. At the University of Victoria, student athletes from out of town couch surf with teammates.

Even if rental accommodation can be found, it is unaffordable and unsustainable on minimum wage.

One of the responses from developers has been to promote the Missing Middle in housing. More duplexes, quadplexes and townhomes in single-family zoning neighbourhoods will ease the pressure on the lower end of the rental market. These new homes will not be affordable, but they will be attainable for people earning good middle-class salaries who cannot catch up to the rising cost of single-family homes.

In the 2022 municipal election, candidates in favour of the Missing Middle won a majority on council. It is not going to happen easily. Victoria mimics the mother country in its class divide. One correspondent to the *Times Colonist* letter page groused that owners of single-family homes will not want densification because they "pay exorbitant taxes to enjoy that single family zoning." Fact check: residential property taxes in B.C. are among the sweetest tax breaks you're likely to find.

HERE IS WHAT the nostalgists and their Britannia theme-park construct ignore. From gold-rush sojourners to 1960s draft dodgers, Vancouver Island has long attracted utopians, dystopians, freaks, bikers, misfits, outsiders, outlaws and hippies.

Not all of those who wind up in this far corner have good intentions. Victoria has a dark side, expressed every few years by a crime of unimaginable horror. We'll refer to them in shorthand to avoid the gory details: Leo Mantha, the last person hanged in British Columbia; Robert Frisbee, the cruise-ship killer; the murder of Shannon Guyatt; the unsolved murder of real-estate agent Lindsay Buziak in what American television described as the Dream House Murder; the murder of his mother and grandmother orchestrated by high-schooler Darren Huenemann; poor Reena Virk.

Little Michael Dunahee disappeared from a playground while his mother played touch football, changing forever Victoria's perception of itself as a safe city. The now-discredited book *Michelle Remembers* generated the Satanic Panic of the 1980s, as Victoria psychiatrist Lawrence Pazder and his patient (and future wife) Michelle Smith recounted what was described as her suppressed memories of ritual abuse. The city also served as a haven for the lawyer Douglas Christie, a Nazi supporter, who maintained an office in a parking-lot shed across from the courthouse.

THE DUKE AND DUCHESS of Sussex stayed at an $18-million waterfront estate called Mille Fleurs. Reporters revealed that the sprawling modern mansion on three acres overlooking Saanich Inlet was owned by a Russian oligarch. If that eroded Victoria's Anglo-centric narrative some, well, the city's downtown no longer refers much to faded empire. Much of the cheesy tourism stuff (the wax museum, the classic car museum, the Undersea Gardens) disappeared as tastes changed and downtown land became more valuable. More condos have been built, so more people live in a downtown once moribund in the evening and all but abandoned during the winter. Restaurants and other businesses have sprung up to cater to locals.

Victoria's economy depends on tourism, the provincial government and commercial activity serving residents. Where once the waters of the inlet called the Gorge were polluted by industrial activity such as milling, now people swim and kayak. We also no longer flush our waste into the sea without treatment. (Thanks, in part, to the advocacy of Mr. Floatie, a campaigner dressed in a homemade costume to resemble an anthropomorphic stool.)

With coffee shops, food trucks, fancy doughnuts, bakeries, bookstores, comic-book shops and boutiques, not to mention an exciting food scene that includes craft brewers and distillers, as well as an influential opera society and a booming tech sector, plus several post-secondary institutions, with a new one yet to be built in suburban Langford, Victoria has become a Little Portland.

The downtown skyline is dotted with cranes. New condo developments and taller towers are filling in the downtown core. The population will undoubtedly continue to boom in the coming years, which will do little to relax the brigades of the disgruntled.

The city is in flux. And it registers the seismic social shifts beyond its borders whenever there is a protest on the lawn of the Legislature. Which feeds the local economy. Protesters spend money to eat, drink and travel, including last year's obnoxious anti-vaxxers in their flag-bedecked gas guzzlers. In some ways, we are returning to the early days, as an Indigenous legacy and presence is acknowledged and embraced, while the population becomes ever more diverse.

Happily, even as it grows, Victoria has not completely lost a certain kind of small-town charm. When people exit the bus, they thank the driver, a practice that was the subject of a viral TikTok video last year.

QUICK FACTS ABOUT VICTORIA

→ Victoria is home to Canada's first Chinatown. The community was founded in 1858. Its Fan Tan Alley is known as the narrowest street in the world.

→ The Fairmont Empress serves five hundred thousand cups of tea per year.

→ British architect Francis Rattenbury designed the Fairmont Empress as well as the Parliament Buildings and the Vancouver Art Gallery. Rattenbury was a womanizer and alcoholic who was murdered by his second wife's lover, who also happened to be the couple's chauffeur.

FAIRY CREEK

Three Days in the Theatre of an Old-Growth Blockade

ARNO KOPECKY

(2021)

ONE PLACE TO START is Google Earth. Type in "Fairy Creek." Watch the planet swivel round to Canada's west coast and zoom into Vancouver Island, green from a distance but gathering grey-brown splotches as the clearcuts come into range.

There's Port Renfrew, the logging and fishing town at the south end of the West Coast Trail; beside it, tucked into the estuary where the San Juan and Gordon rivers spill into a broad bay lined with mammoth driftwood, is the Pacheedaht Nation's reserve, just a few dozen bungalows and trailer homes. Six kilometres east of here—shockingly close—the watershed begins: a dark green U-shaped valley, walled off on three sides by steep ridges whose conifer-quilted slopes drain through a multitude of creeks into a single artery that wiggles westward down the valley bottom, headed for the sea. That's it. The last intact valley of ancient coastal temperate rainforest outside of a park on southern Vancouver Island, one of the very few like it left on Earth, and by far the closest to a pub.

This proximity to civilization has until now been a threat. How Fairy Creek evaded a century of industrial logging that liquidated over ninety-seven percent of B.C.'s big-tree old growth is a mystery. It's a three-hour drive

from the capital of a province built on old-growth logging. There's a sawmill fifteen minutes away. The surrounding valleys were long ago obliterated. But now that Teal-Jones has been licensed by the province to log one-sixth of the valley, the same roads that could destroy Fairy Creek have become its greatest salvation. The ease of access has allowed mothers and students and hippies and elders and politicians and activists and—most crucially—Indigenous peoples from all across this coast to flood into the region, maintain a thriving base camp, and run the rotating blockades that have kept the saws at bay for the last ten months.

The theatre of operations includes Caycuse Watershed, a bigger, more sprawling complex of valleys and ridges and rivers and creeks just north of Fairy Creek that industry's been picking away at for years, but which still has some huge pockets of unfathomable trees. This was where I started.

I catch the first ferry from Vancouver to Nanaimo on May 25, 2021, eight days after police began enforcing a court injunction authorizing them to clear the blockades so that the logging could resume. In those eight days, the RCMP apprehended over sixty people. They got fifty-five more that morning while my ferry crossed the Georgia Strait.

"You're not planning to join them, are you?" asks the officer checking my credentials at kilometre thirty-seven of South Shore Main. The RCMP have their own blockades, playing leapfrog with those of the forest defenders—each new blockade a little farther from the cut block than the last. "A lot of journalists are embedding themselves among the protesters once they get through."

He peers through the windows of my rental car, frowns at the tent and sleeping bag, but eventually lets me through on the strength of an email exchange with my editor I'd saved on my phone (there is no cell service inside this theatre). A police car escorts me and a CTV cameraman six kilometres up the road, where we reach a sombre scene.

Some thirty protesters are corralled on the side of the road, waiting to be taken to the nearest station. The RCMP are trucking them out three at a time, a process that takes eleven hours. The arrestees are given the option of signing a statement promising not to return in exchange for being set free on the spot—doing so, however, would elevate the consequences of any future arrests. Nobody signs the statement.

A few kilometres farther up this road, where the RCMP wouldn't allow me to go, loggers are felling giants. Eight of those giants are occupied by tree sitters, camped dozens of metres up in the canopy. By the time you read this, those sitters will have been plucked out by helicopter and the trees they were tied to will be dead. None of that is visible, or knowable, from this drab patch of logging road where nothing much is happening. That is of course the point.

There was a bit of drama on this spot four hours earlier, when over a dozen RCMP trucks blazed in and skidded to a halt and declared the five dozen blockaders to be under arrest. Perhaps coincidentally, this particular blockade had a high proportion of Indigenous members that day, most of whom scrambled into their cars in terror when the police roared up. “That was good for me to see,” a white woman in her fifties among the arrestees tells me. A fifth-generation islander from a long line of loggers, she is here to make amends; like many other settlers, she is getting a crash course in truth and reconciliation behind the scenes. “It made me wonder what they’ve been through at the hands of the police when no one was around to see.”

A strip of yellow crime-scene tape separates the journalist corral from the arrestee corral, while fifteen officers look on from the middle of the road. Everyone is bored and suspicious and annoyed. Everyone is wasting everyone’s time. The situation feels contrived by someone or something far away and high above. It feels designed to illuminate futility—for the police, of quelling the protests; for the protesters, of stopping the logging; for me, of trying to capture what is going on in the space of a recorded conversation. This was all set into motion long ago, and everyone, including me, is sticking to their script.

I ask if anyone on the other side of the yellow tape would like to chat and am met by dubious looks. White journalists have been oversimplifying and misrepresenting this scene for weeks now, in particular the Indigenous aspect of the story. It's a subtle thing, but glaringly obvious to those on the receiving end, the way so many of us have reported on the conflict between the Pacheedaht Nation's elected and hereditary leaderships with a tone of smug colonial derision. *Look how divided they are.*

A red-headed young man agrees to speak with me, but he's interrupted by a woman with a "Land Back" mask and an air of authority. She is Kati George-Jim, the niece of the Pacheedaht Elder Bill Jones.

BILL JONES has been passionately and eloquently speaking out in defence of the movement, in defence of the ancient rainforest, and also in defence of his nation's right to be divided on an issue that has divided every community on this island, all the way up to the premier's own party.

Jones began speaking out a month ago, right after elected chief councillor Jeff Jones issued a statement asking the blockaders to go home. At that point the blockaders, who called themselves the Rainforest Flying Squad, were still almost entirely non-Indigenous and had already come under fire for not having taken the time to build a relationship with the Pacheedaht. The nation operates three sawmills in this region, including one specifically designed to handle large old-growth cedar; they receive a cut of stumpage fees from the province, an agreement that includes a promise not to criticize provincial forestry policy. You could call that consent, or you could call it a hostage situation.

"We're playing this guessing game between all these protesters and where Pacheedaht stands, and we stand in the middle," the Pacheedaht's former chief councillor, Arliss Jones, tells The Tyee in a rare interview (the Pacheedaht have been understandably reluctant to speak with the press). "So maybe things didn't happen perfectly. Nothing ever happens perfectly. But I'm grateful that the protesters are there to protect the territory against these huge logging companies." That was in March, shortly before her successor, Jeff Jones, asked the protesters to leave. Then Elder Bill Jones came out asking them to stay.

This much is clear: There are fewer than three hundred surviving members of the Pacheedaht Nation, and the press never noticed them until now.

Bill Jones's intervention resuscitated the Flying Squad's moral authority at a crucial moment, just before police began arresting blockaders. Five days before I arrived, Jones's niece George-Jim was aggressively arrested along with another protester three kilometres up the road from here. The entire incident was captured on film: she and the other man trail a police officer as he walks through their debris-strewn blockade; as the officer nears a school bus blocking the bridge's far end, he turns and suddenly grabs the male protester, who resists being thrown to the ground; George-Jim orders the officer to let the man go, shouts that nobody's obstructing anything; the policeman responds by grabbing her as well. He's a very large man, now wrestling with two people, both of whom are shouting that they're legal observers, that this is not a legal action. The officer twists George-Jim's arm behind her, doubling her over, then grabs her neck and keeps her bent while pinning the other man against the side of the bus. The officer knows he's being filmed, keeps glancing at the camera with wide, bewildered eyes. He has the look of a man who has set into motion a series of events he can neither control nor escape. The scene ends when three more policemen rush forward to back up their comrade and a hand is thrust in front of the camera.

Five days later, George-Jim is back under arrest and talking to me, looking over her shoulder because a police truck has just arrived to take three more people to the station.

Everything is happening too fast. Quickly, before they haul her off, we talk.

"There isn't an opportunity to have reconciliation, or land back, or anything," she says, "unless there is time taken to have a relationship with the land, to assess what the damage has already been. To be able to have relationships with our own family again. Like my uncle Bill says, it is our reawakening, it is our spiritual duty and our love for the land that will bring us to a place where we no longer have that division through colonialism, or division through systems or people or places that are going to divide us."

I don't want to bring it up, but suddenly I hear myself asking what she considers the best possible outcome to this conflict, given that the Pacheedaht are themselves divided over the issue of old-growth logging. She's taken aback.

"I think it's a very misinformed narrative to say that communities are divided," she says. It was and remains the Indian Act that created this divide, stripping First Nations of their land, their governance structures, their very children, while forcing a pseudo-democracy down their throats. "Does everyone agree with their family? Does everyone have the same perspective or experience? No. So, like my uncle Bill says, within Pacheedaht, with every other type of band, nation or community, it's a civil war. It's a civil war funded by Canada, and it's a civil war that British Columbia is founded on. Because British Columbia couldn't exist without all this stolen land."

This is true, of course, as the courts have affirmed in every case that a B.C. First Nation has found the resources to pursue—over ninety percent of this province was taken without even the veneer of legality conferred by treaties elsewhere in Canada. "So if you're talking about division in the community, what the division is is colonialism, and intergenerational trauma, the violence, the enforcement, the oppression, everything that segregates you either to a reserve land or off-reserve land—it's all back to dispossession of land, dispossession of your spiritual and ancestral right to be in relation to the land."

I ask if she is optimistic that the current protests can alter the trajectory of events.

"You know what I'm optimistic about, and have no doubt in my mind? Indigenous law. So that is not a protest, I am not a protester—"

But now three arrestees are marched into the back of a police truck and George-Jim steps back among her crew to cheer and sing to them. It takes a long while before the truck actually drives off. When the dust settles, those left behind huddle with their backs to journalists and cops alike, to privately discuss next moves and future strategies. This interview is over.

I DRIVE BACK to Lake Cowichan, the postcard of a town forty kilometres east of Caycuse that houses the closest police station. On a bridge over the Cowichan River, two high-school girls are holding signs that read "FORESTRY FEEDS MY FAMILY." Every second vehicle that passes by honks in support.

I ask if we could talk. They grin and nod, delighted.

"It's not true that there's only two percent left," insists the one who does all the talking. "There are twelve thousand football fields of old growth there," she said, gesturing west toward Caycuse and Fairy Creek. "They're not going to log *all* of it. And for every tree that's cut they plant three or four more."

Five hundred metres away, arrestees are emerging from the police station, blinking in the sun, wondering how to get their cars back. The girls on this bridge inhabit a separate universe. I stifle the urge to pull out my phone and show them satellite images of Vancouver Island. They are fourteen years old and love their dads, who work in forestry. What they know is that twelve thousand football fields of old growth is a lot, and "everyone has the right to protest but this has gotten out of hand." Five days from now, the grown-up residents of Cowichan will turn out for a pro-logging rally, carrying the exact same signs.

"I'M SORRY YOU CAN'T GO TO WORK. You got a right to work, and you got a right to be angry. I hate that all these hippies from the city have showed up, too. But man, there's fuckin' nothing left out there. We're fighting over guts and feathers. There's a shred left, and once that's gone then where are you gonna go?"

It's the next day and I'm on a logging road that leads to the edge of Fairy Creek, waiting for the police to show up, listening to the only land defender I'll meet who knows how to talk to a logger. Duncan Morrison looks like one, talks like one, grew up among them in Sooke, a logging town eighty kilometres south of here. But he makes his living taking tourists out to see big trees, and when he saw the road above us getting punched all the way up to the edge of the headwaters last summer, he and some friends pitched their tents and helped start the current movement. That was in August 2020.

Over the course of my three days in Fairy Creek and Caycuse, I see various groups of loggers gather below the blockades like salmon at the mouth of a spawning creek that's been choked off by debris. Whenever I try talking to them, they get in their trucks and roll up the windows. At best. But here's Morrison, standing beside an F-350 with the windows still rolled down, talking and swearing away. At first, I thought he was a logger himself. "I love yellow cedar," he was saying. "It's amazing fucking wood. But we're not gonna be falling two-thousand-year-old yellow cedars forever."

He thanks the man in the truck for hearing him out. The window goes up and the truck rolls off, and I introduce myself to Morrison. He agrees to chat and takes a seat on the back of a tow truck whose driver is also waiting for the police to show up (that driver tells me he supports the land defenders, too).

"This is a crisis 150 years in the making," Morrison says. "We either act now and transition to second-growth forestry or we go off the cliff. And then who's going to suffer the most? The workers, if those mills aren't retooled to mill second-growth."

I ask him if he meant what he said to the logger about hippies invading these woods, and he laughs.

"I'm a big hippie too," he assures me. "It's an interesting juxtaposition to be in, between these rural resource communities and all these people coming from these urban areas. I'm glad that the people are coming and showing up, but I think there's a lot of things people don't understand, coming from the city. These resource communities are simply a symptom of the demands that urban areas have for resources, and people become disconnected from the stuff they buy and where that comes from. These working men are just working to provide a need. There's a demand, you've got to follow that. Who's buying this old-growth timber, who's using it? Those are the people we need to have the conversation with, not the working-class man who's just trying to feed his family."

Yet here you are, I say. Blocking the working-class man who's trying to feed his family.

"Well," he says, "these blockades are simply a result of failure of government policy, and citizens are frustrated, and action is the antidote to despair."

I ask where his community, Sooke, stood on the issue. "Divided," he says. "Everyone's divided. I'm divided myself. I understand that this whole province was built on the back of forestry, and we wouldn't even be able to go to these places if there weren't these resource roads to take us. Forestry is always going to have an important part in our economy, but I understand that things need to change. There needs to be this paradigm shift while it's still within our control. People need to understand that this shift is inevitable, and it will either be because we woke up and we defended the last 2.7 percent, or because we logged it into oblivion, and we were forced to go to second-growth anyways."

How, I wonder, do loggers reply to that sentiment?

"They just kind of shrug," he says. "The mentality is that there's lots of old growth and we can keep doing this forever."

The science, for the record, is very clear on this point. One can quibble about exactly how much old growth is protected in this province, or how quickly we're logging the unprotected stands, or even what qualifies as old growth—250 years on the coast, 140 years in the Interior, is the standard definition, but it's muddied by the fact that a section of forest might be too nutrient-poor to support big trees, yet still be classified as old growth because it's never been logged. That's why there's such a big gap between what B.C.'s minister of forests says is left and what the Sierra Club says.

But nobody without a financial or political stake in the status quo believes there's anything sustainable about logging the kinds of trees Fairy Creek and Caycuse are full of, trees that range from 250 to two thousand years old. There's no ambiguity here. The old growth strategic review that then premier John Horgan commissioned in 2019, and whose recommendation to stop logging precisely these kinds of valleys he endorsed in 2020, explicitly stated that old-growth forests are not renewable. That was a central tenet of the "paradigm shift" they urged the province to embrace, which Morrison and so many others have been quoting ever since.

According to Karen Price, a forest ecologist and co-author of numerous peer-reviewed papers mapping out the province's old growth, B.C. is on track to liquidate the last of its unprotected old growth within the next ten years. That's how far away the cliff is.

"I meant it when I said those loggers have a right to be angry," Morrison says before we part ways. "But so do I."

He drives off, taking the left fork up to Waterfall Camp. I stay put.

THE POLICE ARRIVE around noon, later than usual, charging up like cavalry and calming down when they see it's just a few journalists hanging around. It's these kinetic situations that set them on edge—masses of people swirling on the road, the journalists and defenders and media liaisons and legal observers all mixed in together; as George-Jim told me, they're scared, too. When everything is calm and predictable, the police become easier to work with, and even seem bemused. The hippies here are strange and colourful and highly inventive.

A small group of those hippies is a few hundred metres up the right fork, waiting for the police with their hands in dragons—PVC pipe buried under the gravel and encased in cement. The police know this. They checked it out by helicopter earlier that morning. Now the daily ritual can begin.

A dozen policemen walk up the road, seal off the arrest area with yellow ribbon, tell us journalists where we can and can't go (the subject of much valid consternation and legal wrangling throughout this escapade), then read the injunction out loud to the defenders and give them a chance to unchain themselves and walk away. They all decline the offer. I spend the next hour watching a special-forces officer operate a jackhammer to excavate the dragons. Each defender has their hand chained inside one. Another six defenders are standing with the journalists behind the yellow ribbon—they've donned the fluorescent vests that turn them into legal observers (ever since the video of George-Jim's violent arrest went viral six days earlier, the police have been treating these observers with respect). The observers sing to their bedragoned comrades, soothing them as best they can—having a jackhammer pound away just centimetres from your fingers by someone who's annoyed with you is a nerve-racking experience.

Observing it from a safe distance, however, gets old pretty fast. After an hour I look up the road. It leads some four kilometres up, stopping five hundred metres shy of the ridge. On the other side of that ridge is Fairy Creek. The place that binds all of us—loggers and police, defenders and journalists, hippies and rednecks and city slickers—together in an awkward embrace of conflicting obligations.

I leave the last dragon behind and start walking.

HOW CAN I MAKE YOU FEEL an old-growth forest if you've never been in one?

We both know I can't. Not through a computer screen. Books like *The Overstory* or *Finding the Mother Tree* will get you closer. But even they fall short. There's no way to transmit the sensation through words alone, and all the analogies we employ to bridge the gap between language and experience suffer the same deficit. A church, a temple, a cathedral. To say that it feels sacred has the perverse effect of sounding trite, which is to say, profane.

And yet: the memory that springs into my mind when I enter the headwaters of Fairy Creek is of the sanctuary in the Great Mosque of Córdoba, Spain, where over 850 pillars form an ancient forest of onyx and jasper and marble and granite. The forest at the top of Fairy Creek is similar. Because of the altitude, verging on subalpine, there are none of those knotted and gnarled five-metre-wide cedars you find lower down the valley; here, it is all smooth vertical trunks of hemlock, spruce and Douglas fir, spaced with an eerie geometry that maximizes their mutual access to light and soil and water. Many of these trees are around the same age as that mosque, which was built in AD 785.

Clouds have settled in by the time I arrive, and they smother the treetops like a dripping ceiling. The only sound is that of several million raindrops landing on needles. Not even a bird sings.

I don't mean to sound romantic. It's also true that these forests are miserable to walk through, so dense it feels like hands are grabbing at your thighs and ankles with every step—and that's the path of least resistance. It's not a place for frolicking. You get soaked and scratched and exhausted just to progress at the pace of a sloth, without any of the grace. But every so often you can get a moment like the one I have when I sit down and stop trying to do anything or go anywhere or think of ways to change my premier's mind. A moment where it's just you and an infinity of ancient columns that disappear into a belly of cloud like so many umbilical cords, and then you think: if only everyone on Earth could have this experience.

Not because of these forests' contribution to carbon storage and biodiversity, though of course there is that too. But really, just for the rapturous delight of brushing up against something older and bigger than we'll ever be. Something that connects us not only to the past, but to the future. Among these ancient beings there are seedlings too.

THE NEXT DAY IS ATROCIOUS.

Pelting rain and howling wind, it feels like January. I wind up at Waterfall Camp, the best-defended blockade of them all: hundreds of boulders and several abandoned vehicles block the approach to a compound built around a narrow bridge that spans a tumbling waterfall. There is a gate before the bridge, with three defenders chained together right in front of it—they're just the welcoming committee. Inside and almost underneath the gate, a man lies on the ground, one arm buried in a dragon, tarps piled over him like blankets. He's getting pounded by rain and flecks of wood that come flying off the chopping block two metres from his head, as the support crew works to keep a bonfire burning hot.

The road is turning into a creek, sending sheets of water directly into the prone defender until one of the support crew—the chief of staff for a sympathetic member of Parliament—digs a trench around his body to divert the flow. Farther along, on the far side of the bonfire, another man lies half under a school bus, also chained to a dragon. Next, on the bridge, a woman dangles in a harness three metres up in the crook of a huge log tripod. Beside her tripod, a minivan is parked in such a way that one tire wedges down the end of a sailboat's aluminum mast; the mast stretches perpendicular across the bridge and juts off the side of the mountain, out into space, high above the jagged rocks of the raging waterfall. A man sits at the end of the mast. If he slips, or if the van holding the mast in place is pushed half a foot forward or backward, he will crash to his death.

The wind and rain are picking up and the waterfall is pounding harder every thirty minutes. A police helicopter sweeps overhead and hovers there awhile, just as the CBC reporter up here with me tries to interview the man at the end of the mast. "Aren't you afraid?" the reporter shouts. No microphone on Earth could capture this conversation. The man on the mast shouts back, "I'll tell you what I'm afraid of. I'm afraid the ancient trees on the other side of this mountain will be cut down."

Everyone knows the police are coming—they'd escorted me to the base of this camp—and that's why they're all in position. But it takes the police hours to arrive. They have to clear every obstacle along the way, removing the boulders on the road by hand, using a tow truck to haul the vehicles out of the way. Meanwhile, we sit or pace around, trying not to shiver. Ten supporters keep busy providing tea and smokes and hot packs, slipping into the bush to monitor the RCMP's progress. They keep the fire stoked, then tie an enormous tarp to the trees so that it shelters the fire, and soon everyone who isn't chained to something or suspended over certain death is crowded round the flames. A Cree woman from Saskatchewan, Raven, places buckets under the tarp's edge and tries to catch the water flowing off, but it sloshes free in a different place each time, forcing her to move the bucket over and over again.

This is the story of the blockades. A vicious updraft fills the tarp like a sail one moment, sending spray in all directions, then implodes with sudden calm the next, allowing pools of water to gather in various depressions until the next gust unleashes a new and unforeseen river to one side. The smoke from the fire is equally erratic. The police helicopter disappears, is replaced by a drone. The road I'd been on yesterday, on the other side of the steep ridge rising a kilometre to our east, has been secured by the RCMP, and industry is now on it, logging their way up to the edge of Fairy Creek. They beat that blockade, and now this one has a day or two left, barring some kind of miracle, and then what will happen?

My fingers are too numb to close the buttons of my jacket pocket. I look out at the man on the mast and wonder how he keeps so still and calm.

When the police finally reach the gate, the day is almost over. They arrest the three defenders chained to one another outside the gate and give the support crew the chance to leave or be arrested; most leave, clutching tents and belongings, making their way to the cars they parked far below. Then the police depart too, allowing the last few defenders to spend the night in peace.

The following day, twenty-nine RCMP officers return to clear Waterfall Camp. It takes six special-ops officers and two helicopters to remove the man from the mast. But the day after that, hundreds of fresh defenders arrive and overwhelm the RCMP's checkpoint, storming all the way to the waterfall on foot and re-establishing the blockade.

The dance continues.

THIS CLOCK WAS wound up 150 years ago. The colonial experiment was the thing that set the stage, wrote the script, built the machine and locked us all into preordained, perpetual motion. You can't see this machine on Google Earth, but if you come to Fairy Creek you can't *not* see the way its parts all whir and click and spin in perfect synchrony.

They wanted the land. In order to take it, they had to remove the people who lived on it. The same forces of destruction were unleashed on First Nations and forests alike—but both are resilient, and refuse to go so easily.

The job is not yet done. All these generations later, settlers are still carrying out a mission so ingrained we don't even perceive it. Us? Settlers? It doesn't seem strange that the provincial capital's daily paper is called the *Times Colonist*. Until it does, the colonial machine will grind on, plowing everyone and everything beneath it, ticking along at two parallel time scales: a glacial pace in matters of justice and reform, fast as a buzz saw in all matters of plunder. Extract, remove, oppress, enrich; that's what this machine was built to do. Even those of us on the supposedly winning end are forced into unwitting roles—the police and the loggers, the journalists and the politicians, even the protesters, we're all just doing our jobs. Of course, that's an illusion—we *can* choose which questions to ask, which stories to tell, which trees to cut, which protesters to arrest, which laws to write. Many do. All it takes is courage and imagination.

I catch the last ferry back to Vancouver on a Thursday night, after three days without internet or cell service, just in time to hear the breaking news. The bodies of 215 children have been found beneath a residential school in Kamloops. Two hundred and fifteen children who died alone, whose parents never saw their bodies, never learned for sure what happened to them.

That was one of 130 residential schools that operated across the country.

There is no distance between that story and this one.

There is one person who holds the key to this machine; one person who can turn it to a different purpose. That is B.C. Premier John Horgan, whose riding happens to include Fairy Creek.

Teal-Jones claims the trees it wants to log in Fairy Creek and Caycuse are worth $20 million. Buying them out, and compensating the Pacheedaht Nation for the revenue it will forgo by leaving the old growth where it is, so that everyone can gather round the table and work this out without the sound of chainsaws in the background—this is such an obviously right first step, so easily affordable, that it should go without saying. Twenty million dollars is the equivalent of five decent houses in Vancouver. The federal government's latest budget earmarked $3.3 billion to preserve twenty-five percent of Canada's land base by 2025. B.C.'s share of that works out to at least $200 million. I am not the first to point this out. Nor is this the only potential source of funding.

The bigger, more crucial and complex challenge is to overcome the self-destructive logic of our colonial system. To be anti-colonial is to break a mindset that has been with us for centuries. That part is much harder. "Paradigm shift" is far easier to say than to enact, when the paradigm in question has been in place for well over a century and yielded the greatest explosion of material wealth known to human history. I know that I, for one, remain in thrall to it, betrayed by the things I say and think when I rush or act in reflex; I can and sometimes do break free, but only with great effort. And yet the costs of not making that effort are finally starting to outweigh the benefits. Arguably, they have all along.

What I think Fairy Creek can teach us is that the struggle for change doesn't have to be futile. That imagination and courage, when tethered to empathy, can overcome seemingly intractable contradictions. The blockades were begun by settlers who faced impossible odds and failed at first to build some vital relationships. But those relationships *are* being built, and now Indigenous leadership is asserting itself. That leadership can and should speak for itself. Their stories aren't mine to tell. But I can urge us all to listen.

This process might have started 150 years ago, but it won't last another 150. Here comes the cliff. We can slow down and shift course of our own free will, or we can plummet into the abyss and see how it feels when the machine finally arrives for us.

QUICK FACTS ABOUT FAIRY CREEK

→ The RCMP arrested 1,188 people at Fairy Creek for violating a court injunction by blocking a road meant to give logging company Teal-Jones access to old-growth forests.

→ The watershed is home to the endangered western screech owl, and radar surveys by the Wilderness Committee in July 2021 sighted endangered marbled murrelets, the squat forest and sea birds that fish along the Pacific coast.

→ Massive ancient trees, like the yellow cedar and Douglas fir, are found in the Fairy Creek Watershed. These trees are up to two thousand years old and can reach nearly three metres in width.

PORT ALBERNI

"Residential School Perverted Everything That Was Beautiful"

MEGHAN MAST

(2021)

FOR YEARS, GINA LAING followed her grandmothers up the river behind the cannery to bathe. They walked along a little creek to a waterfall that poured into a clear green pond. A canopy of trees and ferns shaded the women as they slipped, fully clothed, into the water. How noble and then comical they looked when they emerged again—arms in the shape of a V, hands turned upwards, clothes plastered to their skin, their long black braids dripping.

Both grandmothers were gone now. And that memory seemed far away as Laing, at seventeen, pushed her way through the trees. She had returned from residential school a year earlier. Stepping over the stones, she walked closer to the rushing water. She sat down on a large rock and studied the gun in her lap. Her last living grandmother had just died. The only person who loved her "without conditions." Slowly, she lifted the heavy, metal object to her mouth.

Just then, she heard a noise that made her look up. A blue heron hurtled through the sky, squawking wildly before bellyflopping into the water, legs and wings splayed. Screeching and hollering, the bird climbed onto a rock and shook itself off.

"I couldn't help it. I started laughing," she remembers. "I put the gun down. I started laughing. I started crying. I

started laughing. I started crying. I figured, 'Well, if you can be so ugly and awkward and fall all over the place and pick yourself up, I can do the same.'"

Gina Laing is now in her seventies. A gentle woman with a warm manner and a penchant for flower-print shirts, she's a mother, a grandmother and a great-grandmother. She watches Jim Carrey's *Liar Liar* when she's upset, or a Burt Lancaster movie where "the good guys always win." She also likes horror movies because she needs "to believe that there are things more terrible than what happened."

Laing, from the Uchucklesaht Tribe, was one of an estimated 150,000 Indigenous children across Canada brought to residential schools between 1876 and 1996, when the last federally run school closed. Children were taken from their parents, often forcibly, and banned from speaking their languages. The schools were part of a federal assimilation policy to integrate Indigenous people into white society. The goal was to "kill the Indian" in the child.

In the ten years she spent at Alberni Indian Residential School, Laing, like many former students, suffered repeated sexual and physical abuse. She was seven when she arrived. "Residential school perverted everything that was beautiful," she says. Water had always been sacred to her family. But bath time at residential school remains a traumatic memory. Laing would sit in the recycled, cloudy bathwater while staff scrubbed her until her skin was red and sore, calling her "a dirty little Indian."

Over time, she has come to love the water again. She doesn't have the strength to walk to the spot where her grandmothers bathed, but she uses her time in the shower to pray "to God." Though, she stresses, "I don't have to call him God if I don't want to." She reads the Bible every night before bed. Something she learned from her mother, she says, not from residential school.

The Truth and Reconciliation Commission, which gathered witness testimonies from seven thousand residential school survivors and their families beginning in 2009, issued its final report in December 2015. It included a section on "Missing Children and Unmarked Burials."

The commission held gatherings in small cities and several national events in major cities. Closing events in Ottawa featured a walk for reconciliation, traditional ceremonies, cultural performances and survivor sharing circles. The aim was to address the suffering of survivors and to educate the Canadian public about residential schools.

As the commission travelled across Canada, stories of abuse and neglect in the schools leaked into the public consciousness. But the commission did not necessarily represent the beginning of healing for those involved.

It took the federal government over a hundred years to close the schools, apologize and acknowledge the devastating effects on Indigenous communities.

Meanwhile, many survivors began their own healing long ago—slowly rebuilding their worlds, reclaiming their everyday existence through small acts of hope and resistance.

GINA LAING SHARED her story, both publicly and privately, at a TRC event in 2012. She showed some of the artwork she created in an art therapy workshop.

Many of those paintings were later featured at a gallery at the University of British Columbia. It was there I met Laing. She sat in front of her paintings—brightly coloured representations of her residential school experience—and shared the stories behind the angry black lines that streaked through the canvases and the omnipresent yellow eyes. "We were always being watched," she said. Some of these paintings, along with several others she made during her time at Alberni Indian Residential School, are on display at the Canadian Museum of History and will be for the next couple decades.

Laing said she chose to testify at the TRC because she wanted people to know what had happened to her. She wanted to share the pain she'd endured. She wanted to educate people. But telling her story that day wasn't central to her own healing.

Instead, decades of counselling have helped her regain her life. But equally important are the small ways she re-experiences and rebels against what happened to her at residential school.

Ethnographer Veena Das nicely articulates the importance of daily tasks. She spends long periods with people affected by collective trauma, and lived for several years with urban Punjabi families who had lived through the violent riots of the Partition of India in 1947. Through intimate, in-depth research, she studies how traumatic events affect everyday life for individual people. In her book *Life and Words: Violence and the Descent Into the Ordinary*, she writes that when a traumatic event occurs, that experience "attaches itself with its tentacles into everyday life and folds itself into the recesses of the ordinary."

She writes that daily tasks are crucial to combatting unspeakable horrors, because the answer to relieving social suffering lies not in transcendental experiences.

Rather, the answer lies in the mundane rhythms of life.

WHEN I FIRST MET LAING, she was living much of the time in her family home in Hilthatis, a small Uchucklesaht Tribe reserve village near Port Alberni. Back then, the family was commuting between Port Alberni and their village every Friday so that Laing's granddaughter Erika could attend school in town.

Laing invited me to visit, so one day in Port Alberni I climbed with Laing and Erika into the back of the family's black Ford pickup; its cab was packed with red gasoline tanks, boxes of groceries and tuna sandwiches. The Laings drove pothole-filled logging roads with no guardrails for a couple hours, hoping they wouldn't meet a logging truck along the way.

"That's where I used to go to school," Laing pointed to barely visible roof peaks at the top of a steep hill. "Do you want to see it?"

Gravel crunched under the weight of the truck as we pulled up the hill toward the former site of Alberni Indian Residential School. Expecting big, dark, decrepit structures, I was surprised to see several well-kept buildings, a pastel mural and an active parking lot. Laing told me most of the old school was torn down when the Nuu-chah-nulth Tribe repossessed the land. Former students helped pull apart the old structures in 2009, smashing windows and wrenching nails from wood. We looped around, passing each building before heading back down the hill. It occurred to me Laing passes this site every time she travels to and from her home.

Back on the road, her granddaughter tried to figure me out.

"What's your favourite colour?"

"What's your favourite food?"

"What's your favourite band?"

"What's your favourite food again? I forgot," she blushed.

After a long drive, with several stops to admire the view and forage for mushrooms, we arrived at a small dock. A chainsaw screamed from the nearby logging camp, and pop music played from a neighbouring boom box. We moved the boxes down the ramp to the dock while Laing's husband called a friend, from a walkie-talkie, to pick us up.

Laing said her childhood years on the reserve were sometimes very difficult. Families were deeply broken by cycles of abuse. Almost everyone had attended residential school. Laing said the abuse didn't stop once she left school. Her father wasn't around during the summers, when she returned from school, but he was around during the year. He often flew into unpredictable rages. When he was home, she'd sleep under the bed behind boxes, so he couldn't find her.

Her father had attended the same residential school, and Laing believes he was abused by the same man she was. "I remember [the supervisor] hauled a picture of a little boy and showed it to me. He said, 'This is your father. Look how blond he is. Just like you.'" She mimed the way he'd stroked her as he spoke.

But her father was often away from home for work. And home brought some freedoms that residential school hadn't. She could stay up as late as she wanted to, watch as much television as she wanted to, and eat as much as she wanted to, whenever she wanted to. She did not have to eat pasta. The strange, slippery strands in the school cafeteria looked like larger versions of the worms that infected the salmon at the end of the fish season. "I always wondered how they managed to cut all the heads off," she said.

As the boat neared the reserve, the clear ocean water lapped against the shore. The sun warmed the sand. "Coming home is like medicine," Laing said.

"THE BUILDING IS HUGE / with long white empty hallways. / A child walks softly / the echo runs ahead of her. / The smell of Lysol / and floor wax / overwhelms the memory of wood smoke / and dirt floors," read lines from a poem called "The Residential School Bus" from Louise Bernice Halfe's book *Bear Bones & Feathers*. The poem describes a scene reminiscent of the time Gina Laing spent a few days alone in Alberni Indian Residential School.

She had been so afraid, knowing her abuser would soon come for her because there was no one else to choose from. As we sat on the porch of her home in Hilthatis, she faced the ocean as she spoke. She said she feels safe now. Her husband prepared ham sandwiches inside for lunch. Erika, Laing's granddaughter, watched *Into the Wild*. Telling these stories is important to Laing. But the telling is painful. She closed her eyes, tilted her chin up toward the sun and began her story.

All the other kids had left for the summer and her parents were late picking her up. Huddling near the railing, she looked through to the dorm supervisor's room. When the curtains moved, she knew he was on his way up and she'd softly pad across the floor, down the back stairs to the linen closet at the end of a hallway that ran between the dormitories. Climbing into the back, over an edge where there was about a foot of space, she'd push past the cobwebs and squeeze in. It was the best hiding spot. "Just me and the spiders," she laughed. "I'm scared to death of spiders. I used to feel like if they could tap their little feet and tell on me, they would."

The memory of the residential school is "always there. It's always on the edge of things." But, she said, the memory is fainter than it once was. That she can sit on the porch and face the ocean is significant. She used to sit facing the door because that was where the danger came from. Laing was quiet and then straightened in her chair. "This stuff gets to you after a while," she said, excusing herself to go inside to watch the movie.

ABOUT A YEAR after my visit, Laing received some hard news. She was at her daughter's house in Nanaimo when her brother phoned and asked if she was sitting down. She immediately worried he was calling about one of her kids. "I said, 'Yeah I'm sitting down.'" Laing's house in Hilthatis had burned to the ground, her brother told her. No one was hurt, thankfully.

The lawn mower was found flipped over, and the cap to the gas tank was missing. The cap to the gas tank on the ATV was also off, and lying on the ground next to it. The police were suspicious of the fire. It seemed to have started from the outside.

Laing went to see for herself, finding everything in ashes except what was metal. She walked through the rubble and found a few tools on the back porch. One of the RCMP officers salvaged a frying pan for her.

Laing told herself she would rebuild. "I thought I would be there until the day I died," she said. "Then they would pack me out. Because that's home."

She missed the parts of her house that held memories, particularly her porch with the big, flowered Martha Stewart umbrella. But she did not want to be defined by the loss. She began living in Port Alberni, and found that afforded her opportunities she may not have gotten if she'd still been living in Hilthatis. She has spoken to students at different schools on Vancouver Island about her experience at residential school. Her artwork was featured in exhibits in Port Alberni, northern Ontario, and the University of Victoria.

She'd always thought of her home in Hilthatis as a healing place, but says she has been forced to look after herself now. "It's a part of my life I have to tuck away. I can't stay stagnant and stale," she says.

WITH LONG BLACK HAIR, a cautious smile and soft arms, April Martin looks a lot like Laing, her mom. We arranged to meet soon after my trip to Hilthatis. She greeted me at the front door of her apartment in Nanaimo before leading me through the beige hallways and up the stairs to her suite. She sat at the table cluttered with a bowl of frozen peaches, Halloween makeup, school notebooks and a roll of toilet paper she occasionally reached for to blow her nose. Her arm crossed her body, settling into the nook of her other elbow.

She talked about what she and her siblings called survival mode. Even though her mother did not talk about residential school until much later, the experience was always present—saturating Martin's childhood memories. She remembered wearing clothes and shoes to bed. Her mother hung a bag of food and emergency supplies on both the front and back door. This was so that they'd be ready to go if Laing's partner at the time came home drunk. But it was also, Laing had said earlier, because she lived in fear that "they would take my children away like they took me from my mom."

Even outside their home, the family was on alert. "When we'd go to a restaurant we'd plan a path of escape," Martin said. She still plans an escape route when she's in a public place. And she'll often point out the exit to her daughters.

These rituals echo the intergenerational "lived memories" that anthropologist Carol Kidron, who works with the children of Holocaust survivors, describes. During one of Kidron's studies, where she conducted in-depth interviews with children of survivors, she found that trauma became visible through the ways survivors conducted their daily tasks. "The non-verbal and partially verbal traces of the Holocaust [were] interwoven in everyday life. These traces form a vital experiential matrix of Holocaust presence in the private domain," she writes.

Memories of trauma can attach themselves to ordinary objects. Kidron talks about how one woman's mother kept the spoon she ate soup with in Auschwitz—not memorialized in a separate case, but instead in the utensil drawer, using it to feed her children oatmeal every morning.

Every morning this mother uses the spoon, she gives the Nazis her proverbial middle finger. The spoon is used to nourish her children—furthering the bloodline the Nazis failed to eliminate. Small acts of rebellion like this are crucial to reclaiming life after trauma.

Laing, who left residential school in 1964, hardly spoke until the late 1980s. Not only did she not talk about what happened to her at the Alberni Indian Residential School, but she could not even order a hamburger. If a waitress asked her what she wanted, she'd look down at her plate until her husband ordered for her. "I thought I would be ignored or laughed at," she says. When I ask Laing how the server responded the first time she ordered for herself, she laughs. "They got the burger and brought it to me."

On my last day visiting Laing's home in Hilthatis, I followed her into her room as she cleaned. She tossed the blanket to the side and then lifted the top sheet in the air.

It parachuted and settled. At residential school she was required every day to make the bed just so. "We had to pull the sheets so tight that they could bounce a coin off of them," she said. If the coin didn't bounce, she wasn't allowed to watch television on Sunday nights—the one privilege. When she left the school, she stopped making the bed. For fifty years.

This silent rebellion had gone unnoticed even by her children. Her husband, however, began complaining that the sheets were always getting twisted. So Laing, who had waited until she was in her forties to speak, decided in her sixties that she was ready to revisit the old chore. Now she tucks the sheets in loosely and doesn't worry about smoothing out the wrinkles. She chuckled as she moved around the bed, recalling her long resistance. Mismatched pillows created a lopsided landscape. She makes the bed almost every day now, but she does so on her terms.

Gina Laing's home in Hilthatis has been rebuilt, and she now lives between Port Alberni and Hilthatis with her daughter April and her granddaughter Erika. She lost her husband in 2021, and had to navigate a new grief. She still watches *Liar Liar* when she's having a particularly difficult time.

QUICK FACTS ABOUT PORT ALBERNI

→ In 1964, a tsunami caused by an earthquake in Alaska surged up the Alberni Inlet and damaged 375 houses in the community. Fifty-five houses were washed away. Miraculously, there were no casualties.

→ In the 1970s, Port Alberni had one of the highest per capita incomes in Canada. This changed drastically in the 1980s and '90s when a downturn in the forestry industry led to layoffs.

→ Port Alberni is the closest city to one of Canada's highest waterfalls. Della Falls stands 440 metres high and is located sixty kilometres from the city, accessible only by boat.

CUMBERLAND

"This Is Homecoming"

MICHAEL JOHN LO

(2022)

MIDWAY UP VANCOUVER ISLAND, a burgundy sign beckons those passing on the Island Highway to visit the "legendary village of Cumberland." It's a place where the past and the present come together in full force.

With a median age of just over thirty-nine, Cumberland is the youngest community in the aging Comox Valley. Trendy stores are nestled in century-old buildings. The local businesses cater to the musicians, artists, outdoor enthusiasts and young families who have come to live in the former coal town. Some are drawn to the area for its housing prices—for some, it can be easier to purchase real estate here than in B.C.'s urban centres—and its proximity to nature.

Descendants of the early Cumberland settlers intermingle with the new in the small, tight-knit community. But a closer look at census data reveals that one notable element is missing: the racialized communities that were key to Cumberland's history, such as the Chinese people who mostly worked in Cumberland's coal mines, now dispersed to other places, their buildings razed decades ago. According to census data, there's about a dozen or so people of Chinese ethnicity living in Cumberland now, but none are connected to the original Chinatown.

The heart of Cumberland's Chinese community is now found at an annual reunion picnic in Vancouver that has been going for forty-seven years. People have come back from as far away as New York and Singapore for this one event.

The people at the picnic now are descendants of Cumberland's Chinese residents. They carry on the spirit of what was once one of Canada's largest Chinatowns, home to Chinese families from 1888 to 1968.

At its peak, estimates place the population of Cumberland's Chinatown at about twelve hundred in the 1920s. It was a self-governing community with two theatres that could seat four hundred, according to David Chuenyan Lai's 1988 book *Chinatowns: Towns Within Cities in Canada*, and had enough international clout to warrant a visit from the Chinese revolutionary Sun Yat-sen, for whom a classical Chinese garden in Vancouver's Chinatown is named.

THE PICNIC HELD in July 2022 is affectionately referred to as the "45 + 2" picnic reuniting Cumberland's Chinese community—the pandemic put a temporary halt to gathering in person for a couple years.

Organizer Fred Leung kicks off the event. He stands before the crowd of close to eighty (some of whom are wearing custom Cumberland Chinatown T-shirts) and tells the story of how the reunions came to be.

Four former Cumberland Chinatown residents—Bill Chow, Harold Lim, Ken Lowe and Kim Mah—got together in Vancouver and decided to start an annual reunion in 1973, he says. In 1975, the first reunion picnic took place in Stanley Park. They moved to Riverfront Park in East Vancouver, where they are today, after the 2006 Stanley Park storms, and have gathered occasionally in Cumberland too.

People are attentive, but they've heard this story before. Everyone has brought food—Timbits intermingle with dim sum and home-cooked goodies—and they're waiting to dig in and catch up more casually. The group skews toward the elderly, but there are also families and children playing on the first warm summer weekend that Vancouver has had this year. People have come from all over the province for this. The older folks in attendance comment on how the trees have grown taller in the park since they started meeting here so many years ago.

Three Cumberland Museum employees, invited by organizers, are present at this year's picnic to record oral histories. They've brought doughnuts from Cumberland's village bakery and museum family passes for the community.

I'm there too, feeling slightly awkward as I slip into this intimate gathering of families drawing upon decades and decades of shared history. Looking around me, I start to catch a sense of why this community has kept going all these years.

LONG-TIME PICNIC ATTENDEE Terry Leung likes the idea of moving back to Cumberland, but it's not his community anymore. He left to study at the University of British Columbia as a teenager and hasn't lived there long-term since. His uncle Fred, who moved to western Ontario but came back in his later years to help organize the picnic, agrees. "There's not much going down there now, except that they are trying to restore the historic sites," Fred tells me.

The Leungs were one of the few Chinese families that were able to stay in Cumberland after the mines began shuttering during the Great Depression. The last mine closed in 1953.

Fred's was the first family that moved out of Cumberland's Chinatown and into Cumberland proper.

At the age of seven, John Leung—Terry's father and Fred's brother—started helping out in the grocery turned general store to help feed his family of eleven. He took on more responsibilities when he turned fifteen, driving his dad's truck around the Comox Valley for door-to-door deliveries of goods.

"I worked to midnight almost every night, seven days a week," John says. "We were the only Chinese in our town. You had to depend on the Caucasians to make a living. That's tough because the Chinese were stepped on."

In the Cumberland coal mines, Chinese miners were paid far less than white miners. The coal baron Robert Dunsmuir had largely paid for the head tax and passage fees for Chinese miners and provided company housing. Using eviction as a threat, Dunsmuir employed Chinese miners as strikebreakers during the great Vancouver Island coal strikes of the early 1910s, amidst a wave of anti-Asian hate in B.C. at the turn of the century.

"The white inhabitants of Cumberland would come and break the store windows of Chinese-owned businesses after supper," John remembers. "The Chinese were nothing. The names they used to call us—sickening. I still remember them."

"But we had no choice. We grew up, hoping to survive," John says. "Everybody was depending on me to make a living for the rest of the family before I was even fifteen."

At the Leung family home, there wasn't adequate heating and hot water. The *Comox Valley Echo* reported that two of John's sisters died of pneumonia.

Still, it may have been better than living in Chinatown. One of the reunion picnic-goers remembers how their houses in Chinatown flooded every winter with the swollen river. Chinatown was built on a wetland—land that nobody wanted. Its buildings were constructed on carefully raised ground, surrounded by brackish water.

The Leungs were also the last to leave. For a long time, John Leung was the last link to Chinatown in Cumberland proper. A pillar of the Cumberland business community, John served many years as the treasurer of the chamber of commerce. He was named Cumberland's citizen of the year in 1991. But ailing health caused him to leave for Burnaby in 2014 to be closer to family.

WITH ITS ARTISANAL ice cream shop, plant-based bistro and craft brewery, Cumberland today is very different from what it was after the coal mines shut down, when the village entered a long economic depression, starting in the 1930s. You can still find original mining cabins near the centre of the former city's twentieth-century grid.

Chinese workers were the first to be fired in the mines. Without work, the town withered away. Chinatown didn't hang on long after the major mines closed in the early 1920s. Half of Chinatown was destroyed by fire in 1936. Looters and vandals went through the half-abandoned buildings, looking for foreign curios to take or sell.

After a failed attempt by the village to acquire the funds needed for preservation, the entire town was razed in 1968, save for a single cabin, which was relocated to the side of the road. A gun club used the grounds for some time. Today, a section of it serves as a disc golf course. Apart from a picnic pavilion, the rest of Cumberland's Chinatown is now just meandering dirt trails dotted with small informational plaques.

"A lot of people are surprised coming to Cumberland about its history, that it used to be this city with a Chinatown and Japanese section of town that you'd never know if you just drove down the main street," says Lia Tarle, curator at the Cumberland Museum and Archives. "How big it used to be, and how many different communities used to be here."

Tarle stepped into the curator role in 2020, shortly before a large renovation that saw nearly every physical aspect of the museum change. "You don't often get to start from scratch and build up a narrative with a blank slate," Tarle says.

In the past, the museum focused on Cumberland's mining and labour history, with side galleries about Cumberland's Chinese and Japanese communities added on later. The new layout does away with that, instead ordering exhibits and information into overarching themes such as land use, industrial history and resistance and resilience. The history of the K'ómoks peoples and the different cultural groups that have settled in Cumberland over the years is now told in one continuous experience.

That hasn't come without its own challenges. In the textiles section, there's a blank space to represent Cumberland's historic African-American community instead of an item exhibit.

"They moved up from the States, and we have very little in our collection relating to that community," says Tarle.

A museum is a place that holds stories of the past. But it's also a place that holds space for the present, where communities can gather and engage with the complex histories. More and more museums are looking to have "two-way conversations" with visitors, says Tarle—to learn about what they are interested in and what the public takes out of their exhibits.

"Engagement with communities of origin is becoming more and more important," Tarle says. "Not just telling the stories academically from a third-party standpoint. It's really important to learn about history through people."

"These are their families and family history," she says.

The museum was the first to host the recently established Chinese Canadian Museum's first travelling exhibit, A *Seat at the Table*, in summer 2023. The Cumberland Museum is seeking a continuous relationship with Cumberland's Chinatown community to better tell their stories.

IMOGENE LIM REGULARLY travels from her home in Nanaimo to come to the Cumberland Chinatown reunions in Vancouver. She's been involved with Cumberland's Chinatown group since 2001. "It's reconnecting to your roots and knowing where you come from," says Lim, who has roots in both Cumberland's and Vancouver's Chinatowns. "When you have grown up basically assimilating, it's only when you're older that you realize the value of where you came from, and what it means."

"If I wasn't connected to Cumberland, I would probably have a very different sense of who I am." When Chinese people talk about the homelands, a common starting point is to ask which village a person is from. "Our village is Cumberland," Lim tells me.

"You are part of the group, you're recognized. This is homecoming," she says, adding that it's special to see kids come first with their parents, and return later, themselves, as adults.

There's a time-honoured tradition at reunions: the group photo is taken inevitably after some people have left. This one is no exception, especially with its geographically dispersed attendees, some who have just come in for the day.

As the adults corral children into photogenic rows, an organizer carefully unfurls a sun-cracked banner, emblazoned with the words "Cumberland Chinatown Annual

Reunion Picnic." After so many years, it's become an artifact in its own right, he jokes.

The pictures are taken and retaken with multiple devices, everyone wanting a piece of memory to take home. Some leave shortly after. More will stay long into the evening, keeping the memories of Cumberland's Chinatown alive and vibrant long after the physical place has moved on.

QUICK FACTS ABOUT CUMBERLAND

→ The Comox Valley, where Cumberland is situated, served as a travelling, trading and hunting corridor for the diverse peoples now known as the K'ómoks First Nation, who remain caretakers of the land. In Salish, *K'ómoks* means "abundance" or "land of plenty."

→ Cumberland was established in 1888 as a coal-mining town. It was named after the county of Cumberland in England, which is known for its natural beauty—and its coal mining.

→ In 2009, Cumberland planted thirty-one Mount Fuji flowering cherry trees in memory of the thirty-one Japanese families who were forcibly removed from the community and interned under the War Measures Act during World War II.

CAMPBELL RIVER

Fishing in the Haig-Brown Library

ANDREW NIKIFORUK

(2014)

JORGE LUIS BORGES, the blind Argentine, always hoped that "paradise will be a kind of library"—something like a literary labyrinth, where unsettling characters and ideas can happily collide like storied travellers at an airport.

In the 1950s the celebrated writer and conservationist Roderick Haig-Brown and his wife Ann, a school librarian and fiery Catholic, built one such wordy paradise in their home on Vancouver Island.

At the time, Campbell River was best known for its industrial logging and wild salmon fishing, and Roderick, the local magistrate, had just published *Measure of the Year*, a brilliant reflection on love, family, rivers and justice that remains one of Canada's finest and most rewarding pieces of non-fiction.

An early and largely unrecognized Canadian version of the renowned U.S. writer Wendell Berry, Roderick thought that if you liked reading books, "a library begins to happen to you."

Well, one happened to Roderick and Ann, lovers of books. Their collection eventually grew into a special room with ceiling-high shelves containing three thousand volumes in red, green and gold.

Paisley drapes and a fireplace bedecked with a wooden orca carving by Sam Henderson add to the decor;

there is a pipe rack on Haig-Brown's desk, and lots of fly fishing gear. (Roderick wrote about fishing the way William Blake wrote about God.)

Over the years the library kept on happening, even after Roderick died of a heart attack in 1976. Its growth came to a halt with Ann's passing in 1990. Yet its lively contents continue to enrich any humble reader, the way a cold river nourishes young salmon.

Browsing through the remarkable collection, which contains everything from Plutarch to Rudyard Kipling, is a bit like fishing. You never know if you'll catch anything as worthy as wisdom, experience or even a long-lost feeling. Haig-Brown knew that only a rare book (and a rare fish) could change a life, and that a poor one added nothing to it.

In any case no respectable fisherman would ever describe an afternoon without a catch as an afternoon ill spent. A good library, much like the flow of a river, suspends time and invites the idle wader to subversively reflect on lives fully lived, or engage in, as Haig-Brown writes in *Measure of the Year,* "gentle study without excessive purpose."

This probably explains why high-tech industrial societies hold no more respect for libraries than they do rivers. Memories, not shaped by machines, remain dangerous freedoms.

Last winter I had the privilege to serve as the writer in residence at the Haig-Brown house. The library, now lovingly managed by the Museum at Campbell River, called to me on a regular basis, and I often disappeared at all hours of the day and night to go book fishing.

SOME OF MY ILLUMINATING and random catches suggest, as Haig-Brown put it, that a good library "resembles a deep pool in a river, whose depths move slowly."

In these depths I first grabbed an original copy of William Shirer's *Berlin Diary* (Alfred Knopf, 1942).

Stationed in Hitler's Germany between 1934 and 1941, the famous CBS correspondent watched, in disbelief, as the middle class drank the poison of fascist propaganda and became hostages to moral cowardice.

The Nazis, much like contemporary governments today, even asked the correspondent to "report on affairs in Germany without attempting to interpret them."

Berlin Diary reveals all the sordid goings-on that German censors wouldn't allow Shirer to put on radio. Tellingly, much of the book chronicles the relentless and industrial abuse of language.

Before trashing most of Europe, the Nazis cleverly declared, for example, that "we want peace with equal rights and security for all." And when the Germans invaded Poland, Hitler's wordsmiths called it a "counter attack." Words had "no meaning" for Hitler, reported Shirer.

A good cast away from *Berlin Diary*, I found a dusty old copy of *The Wild North Land* by William Francis Butler (Porter and Coates, 1874).

Written after Butler's *The Great Lone Land*, another neglected Canadian classic, this volume breathes frost, Cree and aspens.

From 1872 to 1873, the soldier—a Canadian version of Lewis and Clark combined into one singular Irishman—took a long northern walk from Fort Garry, Manitoba, to Fort Chipewyan, Alberta, and then on to Quesnel, B.C.

As Butler walked, he noticed that civilization or what passed for it—then the machine-made boot and two-cent newspaper—"rolls with queer strides across the American continent."

At the Forks of the Athabasca River, at the time a global outpost for the fur trade, Butler and his party stopped to refresh themselves one cold March with tea, cakes, sweet pemmican, moose steaks, salmon and even peaches and pears.

Ironically, Butler paid for the trip by selling oil-rich land near Petrolia, Ontario. During his walkabout, the captain again spotted the resource that would later transform Canada's character so irrevocably 140 years later: "From bank to bank fully six hundred yards of snow lay spread over the rough frozen surface: and at times, where the prairie plateau approached the river's edge, black bitumen oozed out of the clayey bank, and the scent of tar was strong upon the frosty air."

ANOTHER NIGHT, my hand landed on *The Discourses of Epictetus*, translated by George Long (A.L. Burt Company Home Library Collection, 1877). The great enslaved Greek philosopher, known for his anti-materialist discourses, seems more relevant with the passing of every day. A library without Epictetus is a B.C. river without trout.

While browsing, for example, I spotted this salient advice: "As you would not choose to sail in a large and decorated and gold-laden ship (or ship ornamented with gold), and to be drowned; so do not choose to dwell in a large and costly house and to be disturbed by cares."

Epictetus also knowingly wrote that "every place is safe to him who lives with justice."

Soon a 1948 copy of *Our Plundered Planet* landed on my lap.

Fairfield Osborn, the president of the New York Zoological Society, declared in this book that humans had royally fucked up: they "had become such an earth changing force that they had completely disrupted the symphony of Nature."

He didn't view technology as a saviour either. "Technologists may outdo themselves in the creation of artificial substitutes for natural subsistence—but they cannot offset the present terrific attack upon the natural life-giving elements of the earth."

Osborn offered one solution: people must temper their demand "and use and conserve the natural living resources of this earth in a manner that alone can provide for the continuation of civilization."

Haig-Brown often lamented our careless spending of resources too. Underneath a wood table, I found a large, two-foot-long binder with an engraving by the artist Bill Reid. The binder contained a collection of fine fish prints as well as a beautiful copy of Haig-Brown's *The Salmon*, published in 1974 by the Fisheries and Marine Service of Environment Canada.

"If weakness and indecision allow the salmons, in their abundance, to disappear from the rivers and the oceans, what hope can there be for the future of life itself?" asked Haig-Brown.

HAIG-BROWN, arguably one of Canada's greatest conservationists, kept in his library two books by his equal and peer H. Albert Hochbaum, Canada's other great naturalist. It was Hochbaum's visions of a land ethic that greatly shaped and influenced the writings of Aldo Leopold.

A large and gentle man, Hochbaum lived in Delta Marsh just north of Winnipeg and studied waterfowl most of his life. He wrote about ducks the way Haig-Brown wrote about fish. His classic, *The Canvasback on a Prairie Marsh* (American Wildlife Institute, 1944), swims on the same shelf as *Travels and Traditions of Waterfowl* (University of Minnesota, 1955).

Hochbaum, who genuinely loved people, wrote urgently about the need to conserve wetlands because he felt that ecosystems, like the prairies, desperately needed kidneys too. Wheat salesmen and barley economists ignored him.

"The time when we start saving the prairie marshes may arrive when we somehow realize that we need these wetlands for our own human race, when we understand that the real concern is not for the ducks, but for the people themselves. Can we continue to be strong and healthy on this North America after we have let the gems of upland waters drain to the valleys?"

Given Haig-Brown's passion for salmon and trout, a special wall of the library singularly offers only titles on fish or fishing. They bear lively titles such as *Grim: The Story of a Pike* and *Any Luck?*

Right next to *Trout Fishing From All Angles* sits my favourite: *The Rod in India (Being Hints How to Obtain Sport)* by a very jaunty Henry Sullivan Thomas (W. Thacker and Co., 1897).

Fishing in the colony, which included hooking hundred-pound carp, required some imperial nerve: "The rain is one hindrance, muddy water another, fever, etc., a good third."

And then there is *Songs for Fishermen* by Joseph Morris and St. Clair Adams. Published in 1922, the book contains just about every poem and song ever written about fishing.

Many of the best ditties, such as "The First Worm," are by that ever-prolific poet, Anonymous:

This morning as I went to work
(For work I was not wishing),
A worm crawled briskly out and said:
"Come on, let's go a-fishing."

Inside this treasure of a book rested a handwritten card by Haig-Brown himself that contained another anonymous poem, "The Fisherman's Lament":

Sometimes too early,
Sometimes too late,
Sometimes no water,

Sometimes in spate,
Sometimes too dirty,
Sometimes too dear,
There's always something wrong,
When I'm fishing here.

But no reader could ever make such a lament in the Haig-Brown library.

Here, the fishing miraculously improves with age because libraries, like a well-told story, never grow old.

QUICK FACTS ABOUT CAMPBELL RIVER

→ In the 1920s, Campbell River was a popular location for fishing salmon weighing more than thirty pounds—also known as tyee.

→ Roderick Haig-Brown is the namesake of a large residence hall at the University of Victoria.

→ In 1958 Seymour Narrows, near Campbell River, was the site of one of the largest planned, non-nuclear explosions in history when fourteen hundred tons of dynamite destroyed Ripple Rock, blowing rock and water three hundred metres high. The blast was deliberate—Ripple Rock had led to numerous shipwrecks over the decades. Viewers watched the explosion on TV in one of Canada's first live television broadcasts.

TOFINO

When a Trip to the Post Office Takes Half a Day

KAREN CHARLESON

(2019)

HOLD-IT-IN-MY-HAND Canada Post mail, the delivered-to-my-post-box-in-Tofino mail, is a big deal. We're only able to pick it up every few weeks, sometimes once a month. It's special. Some days checking our mail feels almost like opening Christmas gifts.

My husband and I have had a post office box in Tofino since the mid-1970s. He's a commercial fisherman, and back then he delivered fish, bought fuel and often tied up his boat in Tofino. When we had our first child and began to stay farther up the coast at my husband's home in Hot Springs Cove, we continued to use the Tofino mailbox. Tofino was—and still is—the closest place we could get our mail—and access health care, banks and a full grocery store.

Hot Springs Cove is about fifty kilometres up the Pacific coast from Tofino. Hesquiat Harbour, where we live today, is another twenty kilometres. Our journey to pick up the mail takes us from Hesquiaht territories, which make up roughly the northwestern third of Clayoquot Sound, to Tla-o-qui-aht territories, which include Tofino, in the southern section of the sound.

Faster boats have shortened the trip. In my husband's twelve-metre wooden troller, with its diesel engine, it took more than three hours to get from Tofino to Hot

Springs Cove. Nowadays, our six-metre-long open aluminum speedboat, with its 225-horsepower outboard motor, can make the same trip in a mere hour and ten minutes.

In the early and mid-parts of the twentieth century, there were post offices in Hot Springs Cove and Hesquiat Harbour. Ships carrying freight and passengers and mail plied the coast, serving fish buyers and related businesses like stores and fuel stations. The post offices were operated by settlers who chose those locations with economic opportunities in mind. When those opportunities ran dry, their ventures, and the post offices, closed.

There are no roads that connect Hesquiaht territories to Tofino. If we want to go to "Tuff City" or "Tuff"—the local nicknames—we travel by boat or, occasionally, by float plane. There are no public ferries. What has developed instead is a transportation system built upon a wide array of locally owned and operated private boats and water taxis, ranging in size from canoes and small runabouts to larger commercial fishing vessels.

For the last decade or so, my husband and I have lived year-round at a place called Ayyi'saqh in Hesquiat

Harbour. It is the territory of Kinquashtakumlth—one of the houses, or clans, that make up the Hesquiaht First Nation. Because boat travel here involves the twenty-plus kilometres of open coastline stretching from Hesquiat Point past Hot Springs Cove, travel can be difficult in fall and winter months when storms roll in. There are plenty of days from October to February when travelling across the open ocean is just not a good idea.

I'm hoping my explanations will help you understand our disappointment on one particular day, when we arrived at the Tofino post office and realized that we had forgotten the key to our post office box.

We were well aware of the Canada Post rule: no key, no mail! My husband and I are both well into our sixties. Going all the way home in our boat, retrieving our key and returning the next day wasn't going to happen. It would probably be weeks before we came back down the coast again. We were crushed.

A long-time friend, a local minister, came by. (The post office is a good spot to meet people; everyone needs to check their mail.) He was cheerful and glad to see us. It was impossible to pretend that things were all right, so we told him our story.

"Can't you just ask them?" he said.

We all remembered that the tight Canada Post rules hadn't always been in place. Not too many years earlier, staff could help people who had forgotten or lost their keys by retrieving the mail from their boxes and handing it over the counter.

It was a faint glimmer of hope. I had seen the post office clerk regularly for at least a few years. She had to know my name or recognize my face. Or so I figured.

No doubt, she had heard many sob stories. And she'd probably learned how to tune them out. The answer was a definite no.

In an attempt to forget about our mail, my husband and I headed to the Chinese restaurant where we often go for lunch when we are in Tuff City. It's seldom closed, but it was that day. It was hard to not feel devastated.

I need to back up a little in my story here and tell you about what had happened before we even reached the Tofino post office. That morning my husband had driven our small utility vehicle to the Boat Basin at the head of Hesquiat Harbour, where we keep our boat in the stormy season. His plan was to pick up the boat, anchor out front of our cedar-shake cabin and then paddle ashore to pick me up in the canoe.

But as I waited on the sand beach, I could see our boat drifting across the harbour. The motor had been acting up and I figured that my husband was working on it. The day was calm and sunny, and he usually fixes its problems in a few minutes, so I wasn't too worried. This time, however, the fix seemed to be taking longer.

By fluke, the Hesquiaht First Nation's fisheries boat, skippered by my husband's brother, came into the harbour and headed over to our boat. Eventually, our motor started again, and my husband came and picked me up. We were more than an hour later than expected, but on our way to Tofino as we had planned.

Tying up at one of three usually crowded public wharves is the only practical option for people arriving in Tofino by water. The water at the wharf we use, however, is becoming shallower and shallower as more and more sand settles on the bottom. When we arrived on this day, the only available spot was just a little too shallow for our boat. We had to wait as the tide came in.

A troublesome motor, a boat stuck waiting for the tide—only after almost four hours of effort were we finally off the boat and walking up the hill to the post office. By then, it really was a big deal to get our mail. Except it was not going to be.

I had an appointment early that afternoon with my doctor. I've seen the same doctor for many years, and he's an old friend, so I couldn't help myself: I told him our story of no mail, no restaurant lunch. "Can't you just ask them?" he said.

My husband and I came up with a solution. Instead of going home and waiting for our next trip to Tofino, we could make the two-hour drive to Port Alberni and stay overnight. Our youngest son had recently moved there, and he had a key for our post box. We could get that key copied and then drive back to Tofino the next morning.

We stayed with our daughter, who also lives in Port Alberni. I told her the story about the forgotten mail key.

"You mean you had a minister and a doctor vouching for you, and they still would not give you your mail?" she asked me with a smile.

"Nope," I told her. "Guarantors might be good enough for a passport, but not for Canada Post."

When I first met my husband and got to know Tofino, I thought of the place as a fishing village. It felt like an outpost, really, an end-of-the-road spot where fishermen and loggers and Indigenous peoples from up the coast came to shop, deliver fish and go to the beer parlour.

Today, I'm amazed at my own ignorance. I did not know, for example, that the Tofino post office was built in Tla-o-qui-aht territory, on top of a place already named ńačiqs. Just above the wharf where we used to tie up the boat, there were Tla-o-qui-aht houses where people I was getting to know had lived and grown up. Now they were replaced by houses lived in by non-Tla-o-qui-aht people.

We had our son's key copied in Port Alberni. We picked up our mail, parcels included, the next day when we returned to Tofino. We made it home safely in our boat. Then I had some time to reflect.

Our utter disappointment that day we could not get our mail wasn't just about the post office. We rely upon the services the Village of Tofino offers. We travel, sometimes with quite a bit of difficulty and expense, to reach services that people in the village have right next to them on a daily basis.

When I arrive in Tofino, I can't help but feel like I have accomplished my end of an unwritten bargain. I have done my part. When we can't access services at the hospital, bank, grocery store, doctor's office or post office—even for valid reasons like the lack of an appointment, an already overloaded doctor's schedule, shortened seasonal hours or a forgotten key—it's easy to feel resentful not only toward Tofino and its services, but at the lack of services in our own communities farther up the coast.

About a year ago, an elderly man, one of Tofino's long-time settler residents, asked my husband what he considered a friendly question, just outside the post office.

"Are you still living out in the weeds?" the Tofino man asked.

That question was a bit of a trigger for my husband, a bit like that lack of a mail key was a trigger. My husband mumbled a noncommittal reply and moved on. The memories of poor treatment, of being marginalized or ignored, of residential schools within spitting distance of Tofino—the list is not a short one—are still recent, raw.

My husband keeps a mail key now. I keep a second mail key. We have improved our chances of a successful visit to the Tofino post office. We really do not want to repeat that day our key was forgotten.

We want to happily savour a special occasion. We want to pick up our mail.

QUICK FACTS ABOUT TOFINO

- Tofino is located in the heart of the Clayoquot Sound UNESCO Biosphere Reserve, recognized as a location of unparalleled natural and cultural wealth. Clayoquot Sound is one of the wettest places in North America, averaging four hundred millimetres of rain every month during the winter.
- The Nuu-chah-nulth First Nations have occupied Clayoquot Sound since time immemorial. Before contact, their population reached a hundred thousand. They fished for salmon, cod, halibut and shellfish. They also hunted sea lions, seals and whales.
- Every year in March, around twenty-five thousand grey whales migrate through Clayoquot Sound on their twenty-thousand-kilometre journey to Alaska, where they will feast and grow fat before returning to Baja California, Mexico, to mate and give birth.

TAHSIS

At Canada's End of the Road

BEN MUSSETT

(2022)

THE ROUTE FROM GOLD RIVER to Tahsis, on the northwest coast of Vancouver Island, is a steep, winding "goat track" in the words of one local. But eventually the road stops fighting, slumps and runs parallel with the small inlet that shares the village's name. I arrived at twilight, the water, mountains and sprinkle of buildings barely lit. I had been advised to bring my own coffee cream because you can never be sure if what's found in town is "this year's version, or some previous year's."

About three hundred people live in Tahsis, and for a long time that included noted author Anne Cameron.

In 2002, an interviewer asked Cameron what the aspirations of British Columbians were. She answered: "I think our main aspiration is to be left alone." Cameron lived in a trailer home with her teenage granddaughter, a duo of dogs she called the Pug Brigade, and Brat-Cat the cat. There, she grew pussy willows and tried to figure out whether her latest novel—which, by the time I met Cameron in 2019, would've been her first in fifteen years—was done or not.

And sometimes, when she felt like being with others (at least digitally), she'd pop up in the comments sections of stories that appeared in The Tyee, sharing her

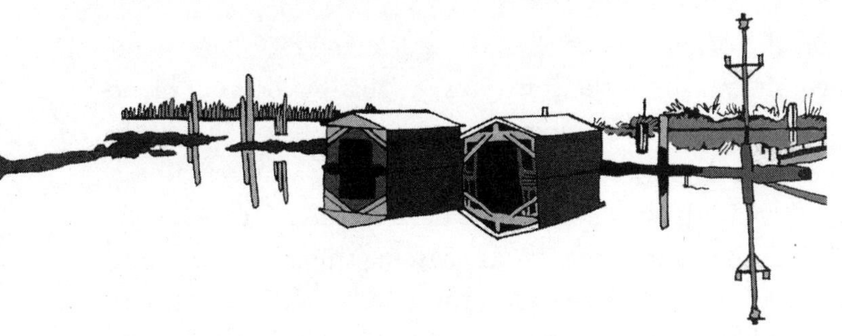

tough-minded, wise-cracking perspectives on what's wrong with the world and right about life in Tahsis.

Cameron holds an esteemed place in B.C. literature. In 2010, she won the George Woodcock Lifetime Achievement Award, an honour she shares with, among others, Joy Kogawa and Alice Munro. She received the recognition for her more than thirty books of adult fiction, poetry and children's stories.

Cameron said that others had preceded me in visiting her in Tahsis, "shiny-eyed" fans who hoped she'd tell them "something timeless and wise." One woman had recently made the trip up from Washington state to ask whether she should continue her master's degree or give it up and find a job. (Cameron told her to keep at it.)

It was a dreary November afternoon—the kind that feels like it's raining even if it's not—when Cameron greeted me at her door. She wore tie-dye, denim and big round glasses that magnified her sharp, turquoise eyes. In a home packed with Indigenous art, she poured me tea that she later joked might be poisoned.

As she smoked hand-rolled cigarettes, she offered her perspectives on many things, including, from her vantage on the other side of the goat track, the city of Vancouver. Its mayor at the time was "a great big bowl of blancmange." Its nighttime buzz was cautionary. "There was just one light after another light, building after building, 3 o'clock in the morning," she said, describing her last visit. "All of the lights were on cars passing this way, cars going that way. And the sound in the middle of the night. The sound coming up from the city is like a huge critter, an animal, the beast breathing."

DAUGHTERS OF COPPER WOMAN, published in 1981, is Cameron's most celebrated book and a continued source of controversy. In it, she offers a collection of stories she says Nuu-chah-nulth Elders told her about the pivotal role women played in pre-contact times, as well as the secret matriarchal society that sustained that precious knowledge. In the early 1980s, the book struck a chord with North America's burgeoning feminist movement. One university professor of mine called the book a revelation, saying it opened her settler eyes for the first time to Indigenous culture.

In 1986, Cameron published *Dzelarhons: Mythology of the Northwest Coast*, a book featuring Haida storytelling. Two years later, at a Montreal literary conference, Lee Maracle, a Stó:lō poet and author, reportedly asked Cameron to "move over" and make way for Indigenous writers. Maracle later denied asking Cameron to move out of the way. Instead, she said she asked her to "stop stealing our stories." An English professor on Vancouver Island told me to this day some of her students refuse to read Cameron's work.

In the 2002 preface to *Daughters*, Cameron writes that Elder women of the Nuu-chah-nulth Nations, from the west coast of Vancouver Island, instructed her "to put the stories on paper and have them published, for all of our children and grandchildren, but especially for the ones who have been deprived of some of the healing aspects of their grandmothers' culture." That explanation did not satisfy Maracle, who Cameron calls a long-time friend.

"What our Elders did not know, and I know no white person has ever explained to them, is that once you give away the story, that is it, your children are disinherited," Maracle wrote in her 2017 book *My Conversations With Canadians*. "Some Elders don't mind that but some do, and that should have alerted the white writer to something being wrong here. Who would give away their children's inheritance if they were aware that that is what they were doing?"

I reached out to Maracle for comment but she declined.

Following the confrontation in 1988, Cameron said she respected Maracle's request. "I understood her point of view." After that, she didn't release a work of adult fiction inspired by Indigenous legends, although she did publish several children's books based on Indigenous legends, including a 1998 collaboration with Sue Pielle, an Elder storyteller from the Tla'amin Nation on the upper Sunshine Coast.

When I first met Cameron that day in Tahsis, she emphasized the importance of receiving consent to tell the stories Indigenous Elders had shared with her. "I've been very lucky. I've had people tell me some absolutely incredible stories, but I haven't been given the permission to pass [some of those] stories on. Stories and songs and dances and poems are the personal possession of the people who are telling them. They're not yours to tell."

Still, Cameron said "at least half" of the characters in her books are Indigenous. "I just don't say so. You know, they live among us, eh?" she said sarcastically.

There's an added layer of fierce humour to that statement. Most of Cameron's grandchildren are Indigenous. In her view, "being First Nations is not the be-all, end-all and final descriptor of who they are, any more than me being primarily Scottish defines who I am."

When Cameron was twenty, she met a French-Canadian pilot. Soon after, they married; then three children arrived. They stayed together for more than a decade and a half. When it was over, Cameron made sure she got custody of the kids and, like so many of the resourceful women in her stories, she scraped by. "We ate a lot of macaroni." Eventually, she sold a screenplay to CBC in the mid-1970s, and then came the books and more scripts and film and literary awards. She never kissed a man again.

ACCORDING TO BC STATS, Tahsis was the second-fastest growing community in the province in 2019, swelling by just under nine percent. That means an additional twenty-four newcomers showed up. Buildings along the shoreline sat empty and boarded up. But, a few decades before, when the sawmills were at their peak, nearly 2,500 folks lived here. In a 2005 dispatch for The Tyee, Cameron described it this way: "It was boom time then, three mills going around the clock, the noise rose from the machines and echoed off the bluffs, back and forth across the valley until I felt as if it was all happening behind my eyes, filling my head with rhythmic pounding."

After that last mill in Tahsis shut down about twenty years ago, the log booms that once crowded the inlet disappeared along with roughly eighty-five percent of the population. The port now sits fenced off and quiet. Tahsis is trying to reinvent itself as an ecotourism destination for summer travellers seeking to fish, kayak, hike and explore caves.

Up and down the coasts of Vancouver Island, other mill towns have suffered similar fates: Gold River, Youbou, Bamfield, Jordan River, Holberg. Dr. John Lutz, a historian at the University of Victoria, keeps track of the decline. He said fewer people live on the west coast of Vancouver Island today than did a century ago. "I mean, capitalism does this, right? At least resource capitalism," he told me. "It has no sense of attachment to the place and very little to the people. It just has an attachment to the extraction of wealth."

Cameron knew this truth well. She was born into a family of coal miners in Nanaimo and moved to Tahsis... well, she didn't really remember exactly when. ("You keep asking me, 'What year was this? And what year was that?' And I will be damned if I know.") The stories she wrote are full of loggers, tree planters and the sturdy women that so often hold these towns together.

"I don't think anyone has captured the idiom of the working-class, B.C., coastal small community as well as she has," Howard White, Cameron's long-time publisher, said. "I sort of think of her as the William Faulkner of the B.C. coast."

Here's an old joke Cameron liked to tell: "God must love poor people because she made so many of them." She laughed. "And that's true of workers." She refused, though, to wax sentimental about workers clinging to jobs in the struggling oil and gas industry. She thought energy companies had duped some into thinking that nothing else exists for them beyond fossil fuel extraction. "When they scream and yell to protect the jobs they presently have, they don't seem to realize that they are at the same time admitting they're too fucking stupid to learn how to do something else," she said.

"Not all that long ago," she told me, "there was a really good job going around the village at night lighting lamps, but we don't have any lamplighters working today, and nobody misses it. Who misses the guys who steered the twenty-mule teams that took the borax across, you know, Death Valley? Nobody's worrying about their jobs. Jobs come, and jobs go."

Listening carefully to Cameron's profane lectures surfaced deeper empathy. She spoke hard truths about what it means to be working class in Canada today, while directing her anger at those who reap the profits.

"When I was still young, back when the dinosaurs roamed the Earth, we all just knew, the way we knew the tide comes in and the tide goes out, we knew we were going to get a job, we were going to save some money, and we were going to buy our own house, or build our own house."

"My grandchildren," Cameron said. "They might inherit this trailer, but they will never be in a position of buying one themselves."

SEVERAL MONTHS AFTER visiting Tahsis, I gave Cameron a call. At the time, Canada was gripped by nationwide protests in support of the Wet'suwet'en Hereditary Chiefs' demand that no pipeline be built without recognizing their people's title to the land it would cross, and their right to say no. The standoff in northern B.C. had rippled out, and Indigenous people and allies were blocking trains not just in B.C. but in Ontario and Quebec. It may seem like a stretch now, but at the time, it felt like the country itself, let alone any earnest effort at reconciliation, had begun to unravel.

As usual, Cameron didn't mince her words. "How many times do people have to be kicked in the head before something happens, like a blockade on the railway?"

"Both the province and the federal government have been saying things and then not backing it up at all," Cameron continued. She concluded that the pipeline protests and rail blockades were "just one manifestation of a really, really deep-rooted anger. You can't keep pushing people around and expect them to just keep smiling."

Canadians are "very lucky," she said, that Indigenous people in this land "are as patient as they are."

Two years after her divorce, in or about the early 1970s, Cameron fell in love with a woman from B.C.'s mainland. They got together after Cameron figured out what she was feeling inside. "I was quite puzzled for a while," she recalled. "It's not like suddenly, in flaming letters across the sky, the finger of God drew a message to me."

When Cameron was around thirteen, her mother Annie became a Jehovah's Witness and began dragging her to the local Kingdom Hall. Her brother never had to go, but Cameron's two sisters remain members of the church, as do their children. For Cameron, "it never took."

Cameron and her mother never discussed her sexuality, but she's sure her mom knew. Did it change their relationship? "No," she cackled. "She had disapproved of me for a long time." She elaborated. "It was a strange relationship with my mom because I knew—the way I knew the sun rises, and the moon shines in the sky, and the tide comes in, and the tide goes out—I knew my mother loved me. But I don't think she liked me."

Over the phone, I could hear the claws of the Pug Brigade tap along the linoleum floor of Cameron's home. It was 5 o'clock, the dogs' dinnertime. "Honest to God, they have alarm clocks in their heads," she moaned, imagining out loud the dogs' thoughts. "'What if she forgot tonight? What if she's forgotten? What if she's forgotten?' And they keep it up, and the little toenails go *ticky-ticky-ticky-ticky-ticky*. It can drive a sane person mad. I'm insane, so it doesn't bother me."

Cameron served for a time on the municipal council of Tahsis. She took it upon herself to file memos on the goings-on around town. Mayor Martin Davis, who sat on council with Cameron, said they often read like novellas. He recalled one about the so-called "crow wars" dividing residents of the trailer park where Cameron lived. Half of the residents were feeding the crows, encouraging them to flock to the trailer park. The birds would peck on the metal roofs of the homes in hopes of being fed. This, naturally, irritated the other half of the residents, some of whom, according to Davis, "were actually trying to shoot the crows." Whose side was Cameron on? "She was pro-crow," Davis said with a laugh.

I asked Cameron how she expected to be remembered. Predictably, she demurred. "I'm not sure that I'll be remembered. I don't think we should make a big point of remembering anybody. We should maybe just put all our energy into making things better for the next bunch 'cause God knows the world is fucked, Ben."

But Cameron didn't think Tahsis was fucked, and that's why she stayed until November 30, 2022, the day she died at the age of eighty-four.

"I really like it here," she said the last time we spoke, after the coronavirus had arrived in Canada, intruding even on life where the road runs out at the far western edge of the country. "I've got a few good friends who do things like come to the door with a quart of delicious, homemade stew and just pass it through and say, 'I'm not coming in because if you're not contagious, I probably am. I hope this stamps your appetite. You take care of yourself, and if you need anything, phone me.'"

"That's why I live in Tahsis. 'Cause I'm not sure that that would happen in North Vancouver."

Actually, I said, that sort of thing did seem to be happening in the big city in response to the pandemic.

"Might be doing us a favour," she joked.

I told her about the posters people have put up around Vancouver offering to deliver groceries to elderly people in self-isolation.

"It would be nice if that turned into business as usual when the panic is over," she said.

Then she told me she had to get off the phone. The "fire-breathing dragon" who lived in her back was acting up again. "Look after yourself, Ben, and phone your mom."

QUICK FACTS ABOUT TAHSIS

→ The Nuu-chah-nulth, whose traditional territory includes Nootka Sound and Tahsis, specialized in whaling, and were the first Indigenous people in what is currently known as British Columbia to meet Europeans.

→ In 1792, Governor Juan Francisco de la Bodega y Quadra of Spain, Captain George Vancouver of England and Nuu-chah-nulth Chief Maquinna met at Tahsis to discuss control of the trade and navigation of the Northwest Coast.

→ For three years, Englishman John Rodgers Jewitt was held as a slave by Chief Maquinna, who attacked the fur-trade ship *Boston* in March 1803. Jewitt was one of two to survive the attack because Maquinna deemed his skills as an armourer valuable. After his release and return to England, he wrote a memoir: *A Narrative of the Adventures and Sufferings of John R. Jewitt.*

SAN JOSEF BAY

The Riddle of the Monkey Puzzle Tree

NEIL GRIFFIN

(2022)

AT THE NORTHERN TIP of Vancouver Island there is an unlikely kind of Eden. It is a refuge for rare plants from around the world, carved from the temperate rainforest.

Ronning's Garden, named after Norwegian settler Bernt Ronning, is a ninety-minute drive west of Port Hardy down narrow, sun-starved logging roads. There's always a sense, on these roads, with the trees hungry and stretching on each side, that given a year or two, the forest will heal over the human-made scratch, leaving only a slim, ever-paling scar.

The turnoff to Ronning's Garden leads to a one-lane avenue, more rut than road. Grass grows in the middle, with muddy wallows on each side. It's the terminus of a never-finished wagon trail meant for settlers and left now mostly to nature. Handmade maps show the cosmopolitan nature of Ronning's Eden: bamboo and eucalyptus groves, Japanese maples, Irish yew and Portuguese laurel. It's a wonder what local Roosevelt elk make of it, stumbling out of the woods and into an international all-you-can-eat buffet.

Flanking the entrance road for most of the garden's life have been two specimens of an easily recognized, if underappreciated tree—a Chilean import with a

world-spanning passport and a history dating back more than two hundred million years. It's called the monkey puzzle tree.

You don't have to be an expert dendrophile to pick a monkey puzzle tree out of a lineup. Juvenile trees look like the product of a child's arts-and-crafts session. Rigid branches curl off the trunk at sharp angles, like hand-twisted pipe cleaners.

There is almost an artifice about them, as in amateur nature drawings, where the beginner artist tries too hard to control the natural sweep of a tree's branches, and instead accidentally creates something overdetermined. With its awkwardly jutting branches, and its trunk and limbs scaled with sharp, spade-shaped green leaves, the adolescence of a monkey puzzle tree seems like an uncomfortable one.

Fortunately, as happens often in stories and occasionally in life, *Araucaria araucana* grows into itself with grace, the arboreal equivalent of Hans Christian Andersen's ugly duckling. A mature monkey puzzle tree punches straight up on a relatively thin trunk, scraping the underbelly of the sky at forty metres: tall enough to peer comfortably into the top-floor windows of the Empress Hotel. The branches remain stiff and scaled in green, but they sweep in bold and certain lines: the tree as avant-garde art.

Adult trees are uncommon on Vancouver Island, and fully grown trees totally absent: individual monkey puzzle trees can live for up to five hundred years.

THE JOURNEY FROM CHILE to the Pacific Northwest was a curious one, inextricably bound to the spread of the British Empire, whose ships encircled the globe as if trailing threads of red twine, knotting countries and continents together. In Chile, the monkey puzzle tree is known as the *pehuén*. It is endemic to the northern Patagonian steppe, growing in a thin band in the Andean mountains and valleys bordering Chile and Argentina.

For at least the past four thousand years (as long as human habitation can be verified), the pehuén has been a sacred tree for the Indigenous Mapuche people. Its pine nuts are a staple food, gathered during annual summer migrations, its bark is used for medicine, and the trees themselves act as signposts and markers, delineating family territories handed down over generations.

In Mapuche cosmology, the trees are symbols of community: a male and female tree come together, and beneath their shade families grow and prosper. So culturally important is the monkey puzzle tree that a subset of Mapuzungun speakers, geographically and historically reliant on the tree, refer to themselves as *Pehuenche*: the people (*che*) of the pehuén.

The monkey puzzle tree's intersection with Vancouver Island began in 1795, at the end of George Vancouver's five-year circumnavigation of the world. Following his 1792 navigation of the island that would come to bear his name, Vancouver and his expedition were anchored off the west coast of South America. To the delight of his men, and of the tired and sickly Vancouver, they were finally making their way home to England, though not without complications. At the time, Chile was a Spanish colony, and relations between the two countries were complex and constantly changing. In 1792, George Vancouver and the Spanish captain Juan Francisco de la Bodega y Quadra had met at Nootka Sound, where a misunderstanding had almost led to war. The little inlet on the west coast of Vancouver Island had been a flashpoint for conflict for more than a decade, with the British, Russian and Spanish empires squabbling for control of it.

When his expedition was dispatched from England, Vancouver believed that he was meeting de la Bodega y Quadra to accept English control of Nootka Sound, and to establish an English trading post. Unfortunately, in the two years it took for Vancouver to sail from England to the Pacific Northwest, his orders had changed—the Spanish were to remain in control. No one told Vancouver this, and tense meetings between the English and Spanish captains accomplished nothing in Nootka, except perhaps to give both men heartburn.

The English explorer did eventually acquire more up-to-date orders, which were now to avoid any more contact with Spaniards in the Pacific. Unfortunately, Vancouver's ships were leaking; his men were hungry, tired and growing mutinous. Facing an unpleasant and notoriously dangerous trip around Cape Horn, through the unpredictable waters of the Southern Ocean, Vancouver opted for a Chilean resupply.

For five weeks Vancouver's ships sat in dry dock beneath the cliffs of the colourful harbour city of Valparaíso. Under the weakening sun of the Southern Hemisphere's late summer, Vancouver's men worked the ships back into seaworthiness. Amidst bustling docks, they caulked the hull and sewed new sails, while the Chilean viceroy feted the officers as distinguished guests. The diplomatic decrees of continental Europe were half a world away. They played second fiddle to a much more human impulse for the viceroy—after a long and lonely posting, here were interesting strangers with stories to tell. The viceroy had news for Vancouver too: England and Spain were no longer on the verge of war, and in fact were now allied against the French. *Plus ça change.*

Among George Vancouver's officers was the expedition's naturalist and surgeon, Archibald Menzies. An irascible, red-faced Scotsman with a high forehead and a jutting chin, Menzies was a lifelong gardener and a botanical fanatic. Over the course of Vancouver's journey, Menzies collected and catalogued some four hundred plant species, endearing himself to no one along the way (Vancouver would later attempt to court-martial him for dereliction of duty). His diligence, or obsession, with plant collection lives on among names in the Pacific Northwest, most notably in the scientific name for the Douglas fir: *Pseudotsuga menziesii.*

While his scientific acumen was first-rate, his table manners left something to be desired. At dinner one evening at La Moneda, the viceroy's palatial house in

Santiago, Menzies was served a plate of pinon nuts, the seeds of a pehuén tree. More curious than polite, he slipped the nuts into his pocket and carried them back to England, where he cultivated them in London's Kew Gardens, watching with delight as they sprouted into the strange, beautiful monkey puzzle tree.

In the fad-chasing, cutthroat world of competitive English gardening, the striking new immigrant was an immediate success. Despite its slow growth, seeds and cuttings filtered out of London and across the wealthy estates of southern England, where the climate was similar enough to the Andean steppes to allow the tree to grow.

It was on one such estate that the pehuén acquired its colloquial English name. Sir William Molesworth, a politician and publisher, lived in an estate house called Pencarrow, near Cornwall, which had a young pehuén tree in its garden. One day, in approximately 1850, he was showing his friends around the garden, when lawyer and minor railroad magnate Charles Austin caught sight of the curious, spiny little tree and quipped, "It would puzzle a monkey to climb that." Presumably, everyone laughed with the polite laughter we give to friends who have attempted a joke. I cannot speak to the biological truth of his assessment—having never seen a monkey try to climb the tree—but the squirrels of Victoria seem to have no problem with it. Nevertheless, the name stuck.

HOW THE MONKEY PUZZLE TREE came to the Pacific Northwest specifically, finishing the long circular journey started by Vancouver, is less clear. Possibly it was an anglophilic inclination of British-Canadian gardeners, aping English fads. Possibly some of them came directly from Chile, pinons in the pockets and knapsacks of vaqueros and other chancers chasing the gold rush on steamships from Valparaíso to Alaska. But the best story is Bernt Ronning, and his garden.

When Ronning came to Vancouver Island in the early 1900s, the northern part of the island had seen successive waves of settlement, none of which had seemed to stick. The area was studded with abandoned homesteads, linked on chains of rugged wagon roads.

None of this seemed to matter to Ronning, who took up residence along one such road between San Josef Bay and the newly incorporated Danish settlement of Holberg. A surviving photograph of him shows a man not easily deterred. Tall, thin, with a fading peak of dark hair, he eyes the cameraman with skepticism, squinting against the sun from behind round accountant's eyeglasses. He has a backpack slung over his shoulder, and his pants are cinched at the knees above a pair of comfortable boots. There is a sense that he's been interrupted in constant motion, and is not best pleased with the interruption.

Like Menzies before him, Ronning was a botanical obsessive. But Ronning had access to one invention that Menzies didn't: the mail-order seed catalogue. From his homestead, Ronning ordered seeds from around the world, travelling back and forth on the rough wagon road to collect his earthy bounty from the ferry terminal near Cape Scott. He planted them on his five-acre rainforest plot, creating a bespoke paradise. He also built a dance hall and entertained sailors, settlers and other passersby. Among the seeds he ordered and planted were those of the monkey puzzle tree, very likely the first on Vancouver Island.

WHAT MAKES THE MONKEY PUZZLE TREE even more interesting—if its beauty, human history and biology are not enough—is its deep evolutionary past. The monkey puzzle tree is an example of an informal group of plants, animals and fungi known as living fossils. In a rare victory for linguistic clarity in the sciences, a living fossil is almost exactly what it sounds like: a prehistoric creature that has managed to navigate the travails of time to still exist today.

There are three criteria to fulfill in order to join this august group of organisms. The first, unsurprisingly, is to be old—really, really old. Geologist Derek Turner calls this having "prehistorically deep morphological stability." Translation: not just ancient, but also unchanged. The monkey puzzle tree, for its part, evolved two hundred million years ago, in the Mesozoic era, and has been unchanged since.

The second criterion for being a living fossil is to be relatively alone, on the terminal branches of your kind's family tree. It's less important that the species itself be rare, and more that the species have few cousins or close relatives. When living fossils stage a family reunion, they don't need to rent out an entire hotel to house their kin—a broom closet will usually do. The pehuén's closest relative is the Brazilian pine, or candelabra tree. It shares the monkey puzzle's sweeping awkwardness, although the Brazilian tree's arms stick stiffly upwards, like a frightened, if enthusiastic, roller-coaster rider.

The third criterion for living fossil status can be a trickier one: high genetic diversity. Evolution is a winnowing process—natural selection's unthinking search for optimization reduces a species' genetic diversity over time, in favour of the highest rate of survival right now.

Old and unchanged species, like living fossils, have survived without that winnowing process. The genetic code of a living fossil is the DNA equivalent of the library of Alexandria: it is an archive of a former world.

Coelacanths and monkey puzzles; pelicans and lampreys; tuataras and horseshoe crabs. Living fossils make for esoteric bedfellows. In *Wonderful Life*, his book about Cambrian evolution, Stephen Jay Gould writes that the history of life on Earth "holds a million scenarios, each perfectly sensible." Seemingly insignificant moments in geological time—an atmospheric storm here, a strange ocean current there—lead to vastly different outcomes. Less survival of the fittest than survival of the fortunate.

Imagine a small stand of monkey puzzle trees, as-yet unnamed and unknown by humans, rising alone on edges of South America's Patagonian steppe. It's the dawn of the Pleistocene epoch, 2.5 million years in Earth's past. The Isthmus of Panama has just drifted into place, connecting North and South America for the first time, and facilitating a massive interchange of animals. Megafauna, the giant mammals of ancestral memory, roam the continents. Some of them we know, their legacies echoing in contemporary culture: the woolly mammoth, the sabre-toothed cat and the short-faced bear.

Others are more mysterious. In South America, giant ground sloths roam the steppes. Taller than a bull elephant, and weighing at least as much, if they were alive today they would be the largest land mammals on Earth. Their diet included, among other things, the seeds of

Araucaria araucana: the same seeds later celebrated by the Mapuche, the same seeds later slipped into the overcoat pocket of Archibald Menzies, the same seeds later catalogue-ordered by Bernt Ronning.

Neither the sloths nor the trees have any way of knowing that soon temperatures will plunge across the world, and great sheets of ice will carve their way south from the North Pole, grinding continents beneath their weight and creating the landscapes we know today. The combined effects of climate change, human depredation and disease will lead to the mass extinction of American flora and fauna.

But a few monkey puzzle trees will survive: that single, small population, dodging the farthest reaches of the glaciers on the isolated rim of Patagonia. They will grow in refuge, sheltered by good fortune, until the glaciers recede and they can spread again: first through the Andes, and now, an epoch later, to the parks and gardens of the Pacific Northwest.

AFTER BERNT RONNING'S death in the 1960s, the surrounding rainforest grew quickly to overcome the little patch of green exotica he'd so carefully cultivated in life. At the turn of the millennium, new caretakers forced the forest back again. Today the garden remains a strange, enticing patch of cultivation in the otherwise wild.

Flanking the entrance road for most of the garden's life have been two monkey puzzle trees, the first two Ronning ever planted. On one side of the road, a male tree; on the other, a female. Knowingly or not, Ronning's planting recreated the Mapuche cosmology of the pehuén's homeland: the male and female tree came together, and in their shade the rest of his garden grew.

The female tree has died, but the male tree lives on, and the garden is thick with their juvenile progeny. The rest of the island is too: it's impossible to know how many monkey puzzle trees in the Pacific Northwest owe their legacy to Ronning's beginnings, but he spent his life assiduously sending seeds and cuttings to anyone who asked. By one estimate, at least fifteen thousand seeds or saplings have been shipped from his garden.

Ronning's curious cultivation of the Chilean tree ensured that its imported life in the Pacific Northwest continues, another chapter in the tree's two-hundred-million-year journey.

QUICK FACTS ABOUT SAN JOSEF BAY

→ Pioneers twice tried to settle in San Josef Bay, first in 1897 and then again in 1913. Heavy rainfall, violent windstorms and the area's remoteness—plus World War I conscription during the second attempt—led settlers to abandon the area.

→ The provincial park of San Josef Bay and Cape Scott was established in 1973. It includes 115 kilometres of ocean front, and approximately 30 kilometres of beaches.

→ In 1942, during World War II, the federal government erected a small radar station at Cape Scott. In operation until the end of the war, it was intended to detect any Japanese attack or invasion on Vancouver Island.

BELLA BELLA

Winter Is for Regeneration

'CÚAGILÁKV (JESS H̓ÁUST̓I)

(2021)

IT'S DECEMBER, AND THE HARD FROST has finally crusted into my garden beds and transformed the mazes between wild berry bushes in my yard into a beautiful network of ice crystals in the dirt.

Lately, I've turned to our stores of preserves to keep our family fed, our dehydrated and frozen stashes of herbs and vegetables diligently harvested by my children over the spring and summer and into the first cool months of fall.

It appears that our gardens are at rest now, but I know the deeper work that supports our seasonal thriving is still creating magic in our raised beds; beneath the frost, the layers of kelp mulch and decaying bracken fern, the soil is rebuilding itself with deep inhales of cold winter air.

I live on the outer central coast, where my ancestral motherlands stretch from the mainland through networks of islands to the open ocean. Pre-contact, our Haíłzaqv people lived in more than fifty permanent and seasonal villages across over thirty-five thousand square kilometres of land and sea. Now we are primarily nestled in the community of Bella Bella, facing east from Campbell Island, in a community where nearly half of households are engaged in growing food at their homes and

almost every household is engaged in harvesting it out on the territory.

There's a false belief that gardens can't thrive here, but I believe in abundance. And much of what I've learned about how to nurture plants in this environment comes from watching my non-human kin flourish: grizzly and black bears pulling salmon carcasses into the forest to fertilize the bursting riparian areas, the world shaping itself around the pathways of water, the reciprocity of thinking in whole systems. My ancestors tended root gardens, orchards of wild fruit trees, medicine patches and swaths of berry bushes; they believed in abundance too.

I grew up in a family where self-sufficiency and localized food systems were upheld as an intergenerational ideal, and alongside my parents and grandparents I got to play a role in supporting the food security of my family and our kin by growing gardens and harvesting wild foods—nourishing our spirits in the gathering, and our bodies in the feasting. And now I do this beautiful work alongside my own children, whose small hands gather berries and plant radish seeds and pick peas through the seasons of abundance—small hands that also wait patiently during the seasons of rest.

In my childhood, we spent long days in my grandparents' backyard cannery, where our whole extended family would gather to process and preserve seasonal harvests. Regardless of what bounty was in front of us, my late grandfather had one unbreakable rule: we waste nothing. When we worked on herring eggs or seaweed, us children would patrol the teeming tables and grade out what was not usable, burying the leftovers deep in the garden beds to break down and enrich the soil once Grandpa's vegetables started growing. Clam and cockle shells were crushed to amend the soil, fish guts were buried by the rhododendron, and even the totes of slimy, bloody water left over from cleaning salmon and halibut were poured across the greenest lawn in Bella Bella. Nourishment was absolute and reciprocal.

Part of what I love about gardening is the ritual: it patterns my year and makes me feel close to people like my grandfather, whose ancient rhubarb plants have been split apart and now grow in my own garden. But I also love the sense of agency it gives me. I can walk the linear path of planting a seed, tending a seedling into a healthy plant and harvesting some small bounty that will feed my loved ones. I can deepen my knowledge of our climate, soil amendment, companion planting and other factors that help my bounty grow. Compared to much of the rest of my life, gardening brings clarity and regularity.

THE LINK BETWEEN gardening and mental health crystallized for me in 2017, after the previous year's *Nathan E. Stewart* oil spill, a devastating disaster in which a U.S.–owned tug and barge ran aground in one of the most sensitive and abundant ecosystems in our homelands. Over a hundred thousand litres of diesel poured into an area our people formerly referred to as "the breadbasket of our territory," impacting dozens of marine and intertidal species that hundreds of Haíłzaqv families relied on for sustenance.

In the wake of that spill, during which I represented my nation as incident commander, trauma embedded itself into our community. Personally, I struggled to integrate back to normal life after the emergency response phase ended, and I grappled with waves of symptoms that eventually resolved in a diagnosis of post-traumatic stress disorder. At the time, my older son was around two, and I was early in my pregnancy with my younger son. As I felt darkness around me, I wanted to believe that I was a seed fighting toward light and air.

What saved me was gardening. We transformed an empty lot across from our office into a community garden, building in flower beds and welcoming features that would make it a peaceful space for Haíłzaqv spill responders to rest. We began to offer gardening workshops, using the space to build skills for community members around growing their own food. And the rhythms of being out in the fresh air and putting my hands in the soil helped me to process the deep grief of the spill so I could find a pathway toward wellness again.

We knew that growing carrots and onions could never replace the tainted clam beds or the plethora of ocean relatives that were poisoned by the spill. But it gave me a small sense of stability, control and agency over my family's food security—enough to help pull me through the worst of the mental and spiritual anguish. And I hope it gave that gift to others too.

Later in 2017, in the depths of autumn, I planted a flower garden for my grandmother. I slowly cleared away evidence of the seasons that had passed since my late grandfather, an avid gardener, had last tended to the raised beds in the backyard. Then I topped up the soil and buried hundreds of bulbs in the hope that by May, for my grandmother's birthday, the beds would be in full bloom. Even as I did that work, part of me wondered if my grandmother—then ninety years old—would be alive to see the blossoms.

Happily, by her birthday the next spring her house had already seen bouquets of daffodils, whole palettes of tulips, hollyhocks and freesias, gladioluses and more. She kept the labels from the packages of bulbs in the pocket on the side of her recliner and she'd pull out the worn cardboard to read about each flower we cut and brought into her living room. Each spring brought a riot of colourful petals into her living room, and each fall I'd lovingly mulch the beds the way my late grandfather taught me so the soil would be primed to push up another season of blooms when winter passed.

A few years later, when my grandmother was ninety-four, she said it was time for the garden to be cleared away. She asked me to unearth the flower bulbs and plant them in my own garden at home. I layered them in sawdust and tucked them out of sight. By October, her health began to fail, and although I was busy tending to her end-of-life care with the rest of my family, it brought me comfort to work in my garden in my spare time to put things to rest. I cut up my kelp and decaying bracken fern to top my beds and planted my garlic, and days before she died, I planted her flower bulbs in a raised bed overlooking the yard where my children play.

Although my grief has been profound, I'm comforted imagining those bulbs firmly and safely nestled in the soil beneath layers of mulch and a superficial crust of winter frost. The cycles of my garden have taught me that there are times to rest in the sweetness of grief, to find quiet nourishment in the moments when things are disintegrating all around me—because I've learned to trust in my own resilience and in the shoots and blooms I know are coming after winter, after grief, after the restorative and regenerative period of rest this season calls for.

This is the season of rest and reflection, of deep and often unseen nourishment. So my parting offering is a small meditation: Imagine a radish seed. Imagine its shape, not spherical but a little irregular. Think of its colour, almost like a raw almond. Its size and its weight. Imagine the feel of a single seed dropping into your hand, of several dozen seeds pelting gently onto your flat palm. Imagine teasing one away from the pile and pushing it into soft soil with your fingertip, covering it over again. It'll unburden itself in the moist darkness, begin to unspool its tender roots, push its stem toward the surface of the soil to seek the light. Imagine those leaves unfurling, those roots swelling into crunchy gems of bright colour waiting to nourish your body. A radish seed wants to grow. It wants to thrive.

Rest your garden; let it regenerate. Rest yourself; you deserve regeneration too. Believe in abundance and rest in the cycles that give structure to our resilience.

QUICK FACTS ABOUT BELLA BELLA

→ Bella Bella is also known as Wáglísla, meaning "river on the beach" in Haíɫzaqvḷa.

→ The community is home to over 2,400 Haíɫzaqv people.

→ In 1977, Bella Bella Community School was opened in order to educate Haíɫzaqv children from kindergarten through high school at home, rather than having them travel to schools in other communities. The school is in the shape of an eagle.

ATLIN

Serving the Cranberry Crowd

FIONA MCGLYNN

(2023)

I STARTED EACH SHIFT by vacuuming the grey carpet, which had withstood years of spilled beer, crushed potato chips and creek mud. Next, I'd count the money in the till, turn on the coffee pot and fill the sink with warm water and a bit of bleach for washing glasses—in training, I'd learned that the slightest trace of soap could make the beer flat.

It was the first time I'd lived in a small town or worked as a bartender. When my husband Robin and I started dating in Toronto, I'd told him that I could never live in a place with fewer than fifteen thousand people. Back then, I worked as a management consultant, travelling most weeks to places like San Francisco, Chicago and Boston.

Yet, here I was just four years later, serving beer in a town of five hundred—perhaps as many as a thousand on long summer weekends when the Whitehorse cottagers arrived, towing their boats and ATVs.

Atlin is in the traditional territory of the Taku River Tlingit First Nation. It's the most northern settlement in British Columbia—but you have to drive through the Yukon to get there.

The name Áa Tlein is Tlingit for "big body of water." The town sits at the midpoint of a hundred-kilometre-long lake, the largest natural lake in B.C., made all the

more imposing by the surrounding bare-faced peaks, and a glacier that stretches south, all the way to Juneau, Alaska. Being on the lake feels like floating in a vacuum, the expansiveness and silence threatening to suck your insides out.

While the scenery was an undeniable draw, Robin and I were trialling small-town life, so it was necessary to focus on practical considerations: Could we find work, let alone meaningful careers? Would we make friends?

Jobs, it turned out, were plentiful, which was a good thing, because we needed a few to make ends meet. Robin found work building saunas and decks for people in town. I cleaned houses, mowed lawns, stacked firewood and landed a job at the local bar, known as the Rec Centre.

A thin-skinned morning person who'd have been hard-pressed to mix a martini, I wasn't the ideal candidate. But I was willing to work, so I got the job.

AT 4 P.M., the Cranberry Crowd—retired miners in their seventies and eighties who ordered cranberry juice or black coffee—arrived. They were my first patrons of the day, and my favourite customers. Mellow, polite and always with a good story about feats of heavy machinery, the mine manager who'd won the lotto in 2012, or, my personal favourite, tipping a bartender in gold dust.

Next came younger men wearing hi-vis safety jackets, hoodies and steel-toed boots caked in mud. Each new arrival was greeted at the bar by a round of salutations and back-slapping: "It's John," "Johnny!" I would simultaneously pull a Bud or Kokanee from the fridge—it helped to know what everyone drank.

The town's matriarchs, women who ran the historical society and cooked for the community on Taco Tuesdays, were regulars. They wore gold nuggets in rings, necklaces and earrings, and ordered red wine, which I ceremoniously poured, first into a flagon and then into a glass, from a cardboard box behind the bar.

Nobody sat at the tables if there were seats available around the bar unless they were tourists or consultants from down South who'd been sent to fix a small northern town's problems. Out-of-towners might also ask for an IPA or a sour, neither of which we had.

I could tell a lot about a person by what they drank, where they sat and how people referred to them when they weren't there. Surnames were generally not used. Instead, the town named you, usually by one of several conventions.

For instance, if your job involved providing an important service, you might be known as John the Nurse, Kate the Ambulance Driver or Joanna the Teacher.

Like landed gentry, you might be named for where you lived, particularly if you lived in a historic building. Something like Garrett Who Lives at the Old Morgue, or Deborah Who Lives at the Old Teacherage.

The exceptions were those who had lived in Atlin since birth, or whose families had been here for generations. They were referred to by both first and last name.

I earned my small-town name relatively quickly, on account of my job, but it wasn't without challenges. Improbably, there was another Fiona who worked at the bar. For a while, people called us Young Fiona and Old Fiona, but Fiona One objected, so I became Fiona Two.

NINE O'CLOCK WAS a prescient hour. On a slow Sunday, I'd hear the satisfactory tap of empty bottles and the shuffle of change on the counter, mutters of farewell as I washed the dishes. On other nights, someone would steal the SiriusXM remote from next to the till and switch to an upbeat rock channel, admonishing me for playing slow country music, which I'd found worked a bit like a sedative for my patrons. On these nights my anticipation grew.

I began to count drinks. One, two, three... over how many minutes? "How about a bag of chips? I can heat you up a meat pie in the microwave." Four, five, six... red cheeks, glassy eyes. "How about some water?" Then came the moment I dreaded. "I'm sorry, I can't serve you another," as I braced for a tirade of cursing, smashing their empty glass down, and if I was lucky, storming out.

Some saw the cut-off as an opportunity to negotiate: "Just one more, and then we'll go to bed." One night, I acquiesced, then held firm, then served them another. I lost all authority, at which point, surprising even myself, I broke into tears. They chastised me, but it had spoiled the mood and they finally went home.

On my next shift, one of them leaned across the bar.

"You can never let them see you cry," he whispered, "Never let them see you cry."

I got to know him as the months rolled on. On long, slow shifts, he told me about his life and how he longed to find love. He taught me how to make a plaintive moose call. In the fall, he invited Robin and me over for moose bolognese and became one of our first new friends.

In Toronto and Vancouver, my friend groups consisted of ambitious young women with university degrees who went on leadership retreats in Palm Springs. Here, my friend group ranged from eight-year-olds to eighty-year-olds, university professors to people with prison records. It was more like family than friendship. They weren't always the people I would have chosen, nor would they have chosen me, as our politics and beliefs sometimes differed quite a bit. Yet, somewhere in the space between a thousand tiny interactions—lending tools, exchanging pleasantries, knowing glances at community meetings—a kinship formed.

Like everything else in the North, friendships grow slowly. Newcomers are, understandably, only tentatively embraced because no one trusts they will stay.

The slow change from stranger to friend is maybe best exemplified by another one of my patrons, who I'll call Dennis, who was quiet and new to town. He showed up every night around 8 p.m., ordered water and sat at the bar in silence. I often wondered why he bothered if he wasn't going to talk to anyone, but this routine persisted until I left the job that winter.

A couple of years later, Robin pointed out a man enthusiastically twirling a baton in Atlin's Canada Day parade.

It was Dennis. He was so ebullient I hadn't recognized him. When he died soon after, his many friends gathered around a bonfire for a reverential small-town send-off. He had melded himself to the heart of the community by continuously showing up.

AFTER THE LAST PATRONS LEFT, I unlocked the staff-only backroom, where we kept the inventory, so that I could restock the bar before counting our remaining cash and printing the day's totals from the till. Once, a patron I'll call Mike followed me to the backroom, though he knew he wasn't supposed to. He'd been banned from the bar, but had recently been allowed back. He'd come and go, stopping by a few times each evening to chat. Later that night, when I did my final tally, I discovered that two packs of cigarettes were missing.

The Rec Centre did a good business. Above the basement bar was a community hall where the town gathered for markets, meetings, weddings, bingo nights and potlucks. It was also home to a beloved curling rink, known for having some of the best ice in the North. I was told there was food in the fridge and a folding cot for anyone who needed it. The profits from the bar helped pay for the space and a hundred other little community needs.

Urbanites talk about finding a sense of community. In Atlin, community permeates day-to-day existence. It names you, knows you and catches you when life takes an unexpected turn. It's not perfect, of course. But it felt vital, for Mike, for me. Like drinking water and not realizing I'd been thirsty.

After locking the bar doors, I rode my bike home along the dark country roads. Thoughts and images from the day churned with the rotation of my tires. Dark hills and forms rose up out of the road in the beam of my headlamp.

I still had questions about making friends and a living, and I wasn't a great bartender, but the place was right. I could feel my way forward.

QUICK FACTS ABOUT ATLIN

→ Within one year of the beginning of the Atlin gold rush in 1898, the community was home to ten thousand people. Today, the population hovers between three hundred and five hundred.

→ From 1916 through to the Depression, Atlin was nicknamed the "Switzerland of the North" because it was a popular outdoor tourism destination surrounded by mountains.

→ Atlin does not have cell service.

SMITHERS

All A'bored the Skeena Train

AMANDA FOLLETT HOSGOOD

(2019)

"MOMMY, I'M BOOORED."

My daughter's wail comes like a whistle announcing the passenger train that heads down the tracks toward us. It's 2 p.m., and we're standing on the platform in Smithers, B.C., waiting for the train to Prince Rupert, a trip of 350 kilometres by road that's scheduled to take six hours by rail. Notoriously, it could take much longer. We could be riding the rails until midnight.

If it weren't for the Skeena train being declared an essential service in 1990, the route would have disappeared decades ago. The truncated passenger train that travels from Prince George to B.C.'s northwest coast three times a week is dwarfed by the freight trains that dominate these tracks. CN's trains, loaded with coal and lumber destined for the port in Prince Rupert, get right-of-way, and VIA Rail makes frequent stops to let them pass.

Some fear passenger service here could disappear altogether, despite the train's long and distinguished history in northern B.C.

In some ways, the lumbering nature of this locomotive is part of its charm. Stepping onto the train is like stepping into the past, to a time when being in transit was part of the experience of travelling rather than something to be endured. This slow form of travel is how

northern B.C. was settled; this is made clear as the train slides past the remains of northwest canneries and small communities left isolated when roads bypassed them.

More than an essential service, train travel is a Canadian rite of passage. I did my first trip as a kid in 1983, travelling from Toronto to Calgary over three days. Nearly four decades later, boarding the train feels eerily familiar, and for good reason: the cars used on the Skeena route were built in 1954 and last updated in the early 1980s—some of the oldest still in service in North America.

A dapper conductor in a dark overcoat and cap shows us to our seats, offers us a menu and directs us to the lounge. The last in the procession of four cars, after the locomotive, baggage and seating cars, the lounge car particularly gives a sense of déjà vu.

Its narrow corridor takes me past the doors that once led to tiny sleeping compartments, which are now used as a makeshift office for the conductor. While the route used to be part of an overnight trip between Edmonton and the northwest coast, cutbacks in the 1990s meant the run was severed. Travellers from Edmonton and Jasper now have to change trains and spend a night in a hotel in Prince George.

Our train culminates in a semicircle of mid-century-modern seating, where a curved, illuminated Plexiglas banister leads up a set of narrow stairs to the glassed-in dome car. The car still boasts its original art deco styling. I can almost imagine Humphrey Bogart kicking back here with a cigarette.

From Smithers, the route west is one of the most scenic in the country. As we head west out of town, our train passes through rolling pastures as the tracks skirt Hudson Bay Mountain. This marks our entry into the Coast Mountains and the train rises high above the Bulkley River Canyon before making a brief stop in Hazelton, where both the Bulkley and the tracks join the Skeena River in its journey to the sea. At the small Gitxsan village of Gitsegukla, the train crosses the Skeena, offering brief views of the mighty river in both directions, and we continue our journey through the towering peaks as the Skeena gradually widens into an estuary a kilometre wide.

Along the Skeena's northern banks, we pass through communities like Dorreen. Once a thriving mining town with a school, general store and orchards that produced enough fruit to export to Terrace, Dorreen was left stranded when the highway was developed south of the Skeena. Today, it has roughly ten properties and one full-time resident.

Jane Stevenson, a Smithers-based historian and author of the 2010 non-fiction book *The Railroader's Wife*, bought a cabin and moved here in 2003. Shortly after, her parents, who live in Kitimat, bought the one next door. They travel by train to meet at this remote outpost.

"If my dad had his choice, he'd be there full-time," Stevenson says. But while the isolation has its benefits, it also comes with its challenges. VIA keeps to-the-minute schedule updates on its website and buses passengers when the train can't run—services that don't help communities without cell coverage or road access. Once, when a derailment closed the tracks, her father spent three days waiting for the train.

"VIA used to be a literal lifeline," Stevenson says. "If they didn't see smoke from a chimney, they would stop and check in."

She remembers a time when VIA was known as the "Queen of the Tracks" and freight trains would pull over to let it pass. When Stevenson bought her property, you could set your watch by its schedule—one resident, in fact, routinely did. But by about 2005, she began noticing a decline in the train's punctuality.

That date coincides with the announcement that Prince Rupert's port would undergo an expansion with the ship-to-rail Fairview Container Terminal, which began operation in 2007.

As travel on the Skeena train becomes increasingly slow and unpredictable, it's no surprise that the number of riders has also gradually declined from nearly twenty thousand annual passengers a decade ago to sixteen thousand prior to the pandemic. They hit an all-time low of a few thousand riders in 2020, and appeared to rebound slightly in 2021. Stevenson fears the decreasing numbers will be used to support a case for terminating the route altogether.

"Look what's happened to other essential services," she says. "Greyhound was an essential service and it went the way of the dodo bird."

Stevenson attended public hearings before Greyhound closed its bus services in Western Canada last year. "I remember thinking it's just a foreshadowing of what they're going to do with VIA. They're going to claim inefficiency, claim there isn't enough money, and they're just going to end it," she says.

To make travel by VIA Rail more viable, Stevenson suggests putting rails back on smaller sidings that were abandoned when diesel engines allowed fewer stops for longer freight trains. They would allow VIA's passenger trains to pull over more often and keep traffic moving.

"If CN was to build those mini-sidings, they would not only improve VIA's efficiency, but their own efficiency," she says. "I think there are things that VIA and CN can both do right now to improve passenger service and they're choosing not to do it."

CN owns the tracks between Jasper and Prince Rupert and shares the infrastructure through confidential agreements with VIA. It's unknown how much VIA pays for use of the tracks, but one thing can be deduced: Canada's largest railway company makes for a poor landlord.

Matthew Buchanan, president of Transport Action British Columbia, points out that the Skeena train follows Highway 16, the stretch of road known as the Highway of Tears for its high incidence of missing and murdered women. The National Inquiry into Missing and Murdered Indigenous Women and Girls noted the need for safe travel in remote areas in its final report. It calls on the government to "provide safe transportation options, particularly in rural, remote and northern communities."

All of VIA's routes experience some sort of financial shortfall. The difference is that in southern Ontario—the company's busiest corridor, with about 4.5 million riders in the year prior to the pandemic, compared with sixteen thousand in northern B.C.—expenses exceeded revenues by fifty percent. On the Skeena route, operating costs were seven times greater than revenues.

Out of all VIA's mandatory routes, the Skeena train's percentage shortfall is second only to the Winnipeg–Churchill line. Yet VIA insists there are no immediate plans to cancel the route.

A senior director of corporate communications for the company tells me that the services are "significantly subsidized" by the federal government, allowing the company to offer affordable fares on regional routes. Indeed, the trip from Smithers to Prince Rupert costs about $80 for adults and $40 for children. The same director assures me VIA has no plans to change services in northern B.C.

Leaving Terrace as night falls, the hush and gentle sway of the dome car lulls my daughter to sleep. Floor lighting is the only thing illuminating the glass dome, giving it the feel of a 1950s movie theatre as the train's single headlight projects a display of cedar and spruce boughs that rake the air as we pass.

The Skeena River is known to the local Gitxsan Nation as the "River of Mists," and fog settles into the valley. Cassiar Cannery and North Pacific Cannery, the former transformed into guest houses and the latter now a museum, rise from the darkness as we roll past Port

Edward, a blue-collar fishing community, and grind to a halt five minutes from our destination. Next to us, the container port is lit up like a Christmas tree.

For an hour we're sidelined on the tracks, watching the towering cranes stack colourful shipping containers like Lego blocks. The conductor tells us we're waiting on a train car to move and let us through. I'd like to think there's a mad commotion of yelling, pointing and gear pulling happening in an effort to get this handful of weary travellers to our destination.

But it's hard not to imagine that everyone is simply taking their coffee break.

Just as my daughter's cries of boredom resume in earnest, we begin to move, arriving at Prince Rupert just shy of two hours past our scheduled arrival.

By Skeena train standards, we're practically early.

QUICK FACTS ABOUT SMITHERS

- Smithers sits in the Bulkley Valley, which is home to the Wet'suwet'en people. *Wet'suwet'en* roughly translates to "people of the lower hills."
- Smithers was originally designed to be a large town. Landscape architects designed a street layout that would accommodate ten thousand people. However, both the railroad and the architects failed to think of the soil. The ground in Smithers is formed by layers of quicksand and clay, a poor foundation for a thriving city. In 1991, the town's population hit five thousand, and has not grown since.
- *The Grey*, a 2011 survival film starring Liam Neeson, was partly filmed in Smithers, as was *Eight Below*, starring Paul Walker and Jason Biggs.

DEVIL'S ELBOW

The 100-Mile Diet Goes North

J. B. MACKINNON AND ALISA SMITH

(2005)

TO BE HONEST, we thought we'd cut ourselves some slack. We were going to northern British Columbia, for god's sake, where the fall fair often lands in August. We could hardly be expected to stick to the 100-Mile Diet, our year-long vow to eat more sustainably and reconnect with our food by consuming only those edibles produced within a hundred-mile radius.

Going locavore was hard enough back home in Vancouver.

Where were we headed exactly? Let's call it Devil's Elbow, B.C., which is, in fact, one of its names. It's not quite a ghost town (population: 1), but you'd agree with that description if you heard some of the noises that haunt the eighty-year-old homestead shack we've been in for a month. The place is like a visit to the doomsayers' version of the End of Oil: no road access, no power, no sewage, no cell signal, no running water except for a glacial river. I think we could be forgiven for fudging our 100-Mile Diet rules. One of us hasn't used toilet paper for weeks (ah, the double-ply softness of thimbleberry leaves); surely we could allow ourselves a couple bags of made-in-California granola.

What has amazed us, though, is just how achievable a 100-Mile Diet actually is here on the fifty-fifth

parallel—and beyond. There is a tendency, south of fifty degrees, to imagine everything north of the Lower Mainland and Okanagan as a hinterland of thick forest, early frost and people who prefer shooting road signs to planting vegetable gardens.

Well, we found bountiful farmers' markets in places like Quesnel, Smithers and Terrace. No, you can't get on-site massage or hand-blended chakra-aligning teas, but you can get an incredible supply of good, real food. As a rule, it is both cheap and enormous—cabbages larger than your head, lettuce leaves like serving platters, shrubs of local herbs. (At a farmgate stop in the Kispiox Valley, *everything* we bought was the biggest we'd ever seen, from greens to beans to berries.) Farmers themselves, in varieties from German to Tsimshian to former Vancouverite, point to the rich alluvial soil, rainforest rain and twenty-hour summer days. Others hint at ancient deposits of sasquatch nightsoil.

The fact is, we found more at these northern markets than we have in Vancouver. There is, however, the same sense that most people do their shopping elsewhere. One vendor said she was surprised to find "young people" buying her beet greens; two Portuguese-Canadian farmers simply could not believe we knew how to cook favas. As with everywhere else, the Save-Ons and Safeways do brisk business in organic apples from New Zealand (really—we checked) and processed foods while the freshest market produce imaginable fades into a kind of quaint remnant economy.

Gloomy observations aside, by the time we'd hopped the train for the forty-minute ride to Devil's Elbow, we were stocked: potatoes, summer savoury, celery, zucchini, a jar of pickled eggs, smoked sockeye salmon from the famous Wet'suwet'en gaff-fishing site at Moricetown, cabbage, lettuce, cucumber, green onions, yellow onions, honey, cauliflower, yellow and ribbon green beans, shelling beans. All of it was huge and half the price of either the chain stores or Vancouver's markets. Of special note: tomatoes from Smithers, the best either of us had ever had, from a nearly silent old man named Willie; and packs of dried pinto and fava beans grown outside of Terrace. These are the first dried beans we've seen at any market since we started the 100-Mile Diet, and we cleaned the guy out to pack them home for vegan meals.

Of course, the provisions don't stop as you enter the wilderness—it's just that they aren't lined up on fold-out tables. We had already picked an entire cereal box of saskatoon berries outside the small town of Telkwa (did I mention these were the largest we'd ever seen?), and they kept well, unrefrigerated, until we'd eaten the whole bunch. In Devil's Elbow, there were fresh opportunities:

thimbleberries, highbush cranberries, huckleberries, dandelion greens.

We're far from bush masters, but we know a handful of wild foods, and with our market vegetables and some stocks from past years, we were living well—and living 100-Mile. There was also the old homesteaders' orchard—still churning out heritage sour cherries and apples in its ninth decade, and the contents of the aforementioned glacial river.

Four species of salmon churn upriver through the summer, along with Dolly Varden, bull trout and other tasty fish. Having journeyed rather far from our near-veganism at the start of this experiment, we caught a pink salmon on our tenth cast—big enough to cost a day's wages in Vancouver, though up here most Indigenous fishers won't even keep them. We ate two overdose meals of fish to keep the meat from spoiling and then, on our second day of fishing, lost the rod overboard and contemplated karma.

It's all a swell adventure, of course—good Boy Scout-variety fun. More important is the fact that much of this ecological wealth is neither ignored nor forgotten in the way that it has come to be in Canada's urban centres. Take Margaret Edgars, a fifty-eight-year-old Haida woman profiled in *Northword*, a great, small magazine based in Smithers. Edgars figures she takes close to a hundred percent of her diet from the land and sea around her: berries, fish, shellfish, seaweeds, mushrooms, wild teas and game.

Step off the grid a little and local self-reliance is still the rule. In one 100-Mile highlight, we rode by bike over back trails to trade canned orchard apples for canned sockeye salmon with a neighbour who lives most of his life in the bush—enough so that he has a taste for smoked bear meat and knows how to make moonshine with berries and potato skins (dry, but with a sweet, homebrew nose). Everyone seems to have a backwoods garden, a mental map of berry patches, an encyclopedic knowledge of smoking techniques.

Edward Hoagland, a grand man of American letters, came to this part of the world in 1966, and out of it came a classic book called *Notes from the Century Before*. It was a eulogy, really, a sad kiss goodbye to the grizzly and the wolf, to the pioneer spirit and to creeks so full of fish that one was called Catch-'Em-With-Your-Hand. Hoagland predicted it would all go the way of Pennsylvania and Florida, stripped of wild mystery and lost in a whirl of freeways and industrial dumps.

He was mostly correct, but there's a new possibility here as well—some *Notes from the Century to Come*, perhaps. There are still enough people with actual relationships with the land, especially in the farther-flung pockets of this province, to point to a different way of doing things. There are, for example, people who still remember when commercial farming was a real way to make a living in valleys all the way up into the Alaska Panhandle. (Because of this otherwise forgotten history, our old homestead shack is in the Agricultural Land Reserve… while, farther south, the ALR gets turned under for condos in Delta.) There are still people who shoot two bullets a year, one for the first moose and one for the second.

There are people, like Margaret Edgars, still eating or trying anew the traditional foods taken from the landscape before the colonial arrival of Green Giant and Tim

Hortons. Edgars calls it the "two-hundred-years-ago tongue."

I don't want to romanticize. Rural British Columbia is far from some bucolic throwback to buckskin-wearing live-off-the-landers, and unleashing the citizens of Vancouver to hunt and gather on the North Shore would quickly strip the wild country of every form of life. Still, the two-hundred-years-ago tongue could be our future, too. Look at this province with 100-Mile eyes and it is suddenly startling just how little of our bioregion has actually crept its way into our collective culture.

Take that same perspective into the forest and you are equally dazzled by the possibilities. You see how quickly the first tender shoots and wild greens give way to berries, to more berries, to salmon season, to mushroom season. Move through the landscape as a forager, imagining a culture more deeply rooted in its place, and you move more slowly, dare I say mindfully. And when you emerge, as you always will in B.C., into the shocking emptiness of a clearcut, everything lost for a single crop of trees, you don't think of it as destruction. You think of it as waste.

Well, we weren't sure how long we'd last in Devil's Elbow. But then, the blackberries are coming ripe, and the Indian plum, and we just found a bog of blueberries, and the first chanterelles. Already we have pine mushrooms; cans of preserves and salmon, two (successfully) experimental dried berry cakes. We'll stay a little longer. And when we decide to leave for Vancouver, we'll go home a little richer.

QUICK FACTS ABOUT DEVIL'S ELBOW

→ "Devil's Elbow," the name given to protect this location's actual identity, is in fact the name of a geographical feature of the site.

→ The current year-round population of Devil's Elbow is 1.

→ Devil's Elbow was train-access-only until recently. It is now accessible over logging roads, but visitors still often arrive by train, especially in winter.

→ Local lore holds that Devil's Elbow is sometimes visited by the sasquatch.

OOTSA LAKE

The World's Most Remote Brewery?

AMANDA FOLLETT HOSGOOD

(2022)

"I ENDED UP HERE because I got lost! Honest."

I'm skeptical. The entry, scribbled in the guest book at Ursa Minor Brewing, is surprising given its location a hundred kilometres down a labyrinth of resource roads south of Burns Lake, B.C.

The craft brewery seems like an unlikely—if fortunate—place to just stumble upon.

Indeed, owner Nathan Nicholas says day trippers will dedicate hours to drive from northern communities like Smithers, Terrace and Vanderhoof just to sit near the placid inlet on Ootsa Lake and sip some local brew.

Industry workers have ventured here looking for something to do on a day off. Local cabin owners are grateful for a nearby venue to gather with neighbours, and campers looking for a hot meal and cool beverage are also enthusiastic guests. The guest book even includes international visitors.

But it's also true, Nicholas confirms, that the brewery gets the odd road-weary traveller who has taken a wrong turn.

That's all part of the appeal, he says.

"We really want to have a destination brewery," he tells me. "We want to be a tourist attraction."

I arrived here very much on purpose, having driven 240 kilometres east from my home in Smithers, south from Burns Lake, crossing Francois Lake by ferry and continuing on through the small communities that dot Southside, the gently rolling, pastoral region between Francois and Ootsa lakes.

Here to research an article about the area's history for The Tyee, I'm grateful for a glass of Siberian Express Haskap Saison and a dry place to work on this damp mid-July afternoon.

While Nicholas insists Ursa Minor isn't the most remote brewery in the world (he references one in Norway and another in Iqaluit), it strikes me as unique that pretty much the only thing I can buy with my credit card within a fifty-kilometre radius on this day—save some Ursa Minor swag—is beer.

Nicholas, also the operation's brewer, grew up on this 540-acre property. His parents bought the land in the late 1950s after being displaced from their original home when Ootsa Lake was flooded by the Aluminum Company of

Canada, now Rio Tinto Alcan, to create the Nechako Reservoir that powers the mining giant's smelter in Kitimat.

Nicholas left to pursue a culinary career and later worked in forestry. But he and his partner Gwyn moved back in 2018 determined to start a family business that incorporates the local culture of this remote area.

So it's not surprising that the brewery has a special focus on local ingredients. The haskap berries in the saison I'm sipping were sourced from a nearby farm. Spruce tips for a session ale are plucked from local trees. Rhubarb from Nicholas's garden adds pucker to a pale ale.

Nicholas has even attempted a cottonwood beer (it was far too bitter, but he's not giving up) and is considering a soopolallie, or soapberry, brew. Homemade soda and spruce-tip iced tea provide non-alcoholic options.

"It's a really nice way to engage with people," Nicholas says about purchasing ingredients from his neighbours. "That's one thing we really wanted to do with our brewery is foster that sense of community again."

Nicholas remembers a time when Southside thrived with small sawmills and family farms. But corporate industry made the operations uneconomical and many families left. He and Gwyn both attended a nearby elementary school, which has since closed. These changes left the community fractured.

As they worked toward opening the brewery in 2018, the Nicholases battled an epic wildfire season, which delayed Ursa Minor's opening until June 2020. Throughout the pandemic, it offered Covid-19–friendly outdoor picnic tables and a place for people to come together again.

The brewery operates during the summer months. On this rainy Thursday afternoon, its tasting room is open by appointment only. It has regular business hours Friday to Sunday, and most weekends Nicholas, a former chef, fires up two large barbecues. Be sure to book ahead to guarantee your dinner, he warns.

Other than beer and a hot meal, perhaps the most important thing a remote brewery needs is a place to pitch a tent. The couple is working on that. They plan to open a small campground that will host visitors who want to spend more time in this peaceful location, where swallows swoop and loons call, hours from the nearest city.

"Sometimes I wonder if people come for the beer or to see the crazy people who started a craft brewery in the middle of nowhere," Nicholas jokes.

QUICK FACTS ABOUT OOTSA LAKE

→ Ootsa was once a network of rivers, narrow lakes and sloughs. However, in 1952, ninety-two thousand hectares of the rich valley bottomlands were flooded as part of the Kemano hydro-electric project.

→ Ootsa Lake is in the territory of the Cheslatta Carrier Nation. Their traditional village site was known as Ska-tchola. They were forced to leave with no notice or compensation when the waters rose. The site, including burial grounds, is now hidden under two metres of water. The nation is still working to undo the many harms caused by the creation of the reservoir.

→ One of the first settlers at Ootsa Lake was a Bavarian named George Seel. To avoid being interned during World War I, George vanished into the backcountry, subsisting off hunting and trapping and seeking gold. After the war, George found his wife, Elsie Seel, by putting an ad in a German newspaper.

CHILCOTIN

To the Tŝilhqot'in, With Gloves

IAN GILL

(2014)

YEARS AGO, I CAME INTO POSSESSION of a pair of deerskin gloves through a transaction that involved two parties who brought different things to the table: me, with the money, and an elderly Tŝilhqot'in woman, with the gloves. The exchange was, I believe, a fair one. She set the price and I paid it; she got the money, and I got the gloves, which remain among my most prized possessions.

The transaction was conducted with free and informed consent, a rare thing in this country when it comes to dealings between white settlers and Indigenous peoples.

Ours was admittedly a very small deal, but where it took place recently has become a very big deal in Canada. At the time, I was in Xeni Gwet'in, or the Nemiah Valley, in the heart of a large swath of territory claimed as their own by the Tŝilhqot'in Nation—the People of the Blue Water. (The Xeni Gwet'in are one of six communities that make up the Tŝilhqot'in national government.)

Xeni Gwet'in Chief Annie Williams served as translator and witness to the purchase of the gloves, but mostly she was helping me, then a CBC Television reporter, understand why the Xeni Gwet'in had, in 1989, unilaterally declared their territory to be an "Aboriginal Wilderness Preserve."

There was no legal force behind the declaration at the time, but the Tŝilhqot'in people had a history of bucking convention that stretched back to one of the great moments of resistance in B.C. history, the so-called Chilcotin War of 1864. Then, an attempt to build a road from Bute Inlet up to the Cariboo goldfields was brought to an abrupt and bloody end when several members of the road crew were killed; in retribution, six Tŝilhqot'in men were arrested, tried and eventually hanged, even though they were later proven not to have taken part in the original war party.

The upshot was the road never got built. Until the 1980s, when an explosion of logging and logging roads spread across the Chilcotin Plateau, the Nemiah Valley remained one of the most remote and spectacular (undeclared) wilderness areas in all of Canada. Then, a few years after the Haida Nation out on the coast made their stand against B.C.'s logging companies, the Xeni Gwet'in made theirs.

According to Nen Duh Nen Jid Gwezit'in (the Nemiah Declaration of 1989), there would thenceforth be no more commercial logging in the Nemiah Valley. There would be no mining, no flooding or dam construction on the area's principal lakes, and no commercial road building. The declaration ended, "We are prepared to enforce and defend our Aboriginal rights in any way we are able."

A year later, Chief Roger William launched the Nemiah Trapline Action, seeking a declaration of Aboriginal title over 438,000 hectares of the Cariboo-Chilcotin region. Soon insult was added to the injury caused by commercial logging: Taseko Mines had discovered a large deposit of copper and gold near Teẑtan Biny (Fish Lake) and planned to flat-out destroy the entire lake in order to get the gold out.

The court process in defence of the Tŝilhqot'in people's rights and title—a long, ugly, unseemly and expensive battle, as they always are—ended in 2014 when the Supreme Court of Canada affirmed Aboriginal title a quarter of a century after the Tŝilhqot'in called the question.

That might seem like a long time, but as Roger William said in a deposition opposing the mine, the struggle dated back to 1846, even before the Chilcotin War, when the British Crown asserted sovereignty before British Columbia even joined Confederation, something the Tŝilhqot'in viewed as merely the first chapter in a long "story of betrayal" for which governments have only now been called to account.

The Chilcotin resistance was actually older than British Columbia itself.

"DESPITE THE HORROR we suffered, our story of resistance continues to be a story of Tŝilhqot'in triumph," William said a couple years before the court decision. Indeed, there is no greater triumph in the history of Indigenous rights in this country than the affirmation by the Supreme Court of Canada in late June of 2014 that the Tŝilhqot'in had been telling truth all along.

By my reckoning, not a single deal that governments and industries have done with First Nations in the entire history of this province has been lawful. They have consistently, repeatedly, deliberately and devastatingly denied Indigenous people the right to free and informed consent and have shown contempt not just for their legal rights, but for their cultures, their well-being and their fundamental right to self-determination.

For those of us who have documented, or joined, or merely followed the struggles of the Nisga'a and the Haida and the Tla-o-qui-aht and the Tsleil-Waututh and the Haisla and the Gitga'at and the Haíłzaqv and, indeed, all the First Nations of Canada, including the Tŝilhqot'in—what do we make of all this?

First: this is a spectacular victory for the Tŝilhqot'in and an emphatic rebuke to the swindlers who have ruled and attempted to ruin this province since they first clapped eyes on the place.

But it's hard not to worry that the barbarians are still at the gate, and may be all the more dangerous for being wounded.

To go back to Xeni Gwet'in for a moment, I bought those gloves when on assignment for CBC Television, visiting the Nemiah Valley to report a documentary series called *The Battle for the Chilcotin*. It was the first of many docs I was privileged to do for the CBC that focused on the struggle of First Nations located in what is currently known as British Columbia—the Cheslatta, flooded from their lands; the Haisla, trying to save the Kitlope from logging; the Ingenika and Fort Ware people, flooded from their lands; the Nuu-chah-nulth, fighting for their place in the battle over Clayoquot Sound, and many more.

Those halcyon days, when CBC journalists were allowed to tell Canadian stories to Canadians, have given way to a harrowing hollowing-out of our public broadcaster to the point that, to cut costs, we are witnessing the imminent demise of in-house documentary production. Whose vision of Canada does that serve?

Where to look, across Canada's increasingly barren media landscape, for an articulation—without fear or favour—of what the Tŝilhqot'in case meant for Canada?

"It's Justice, but It Means Chaos" went one headline in the *Globe and Mail*. In the *National Post*, the front page declared "Ruling a 'Game Changer,'" while in the conjoined *Financial Post*, "Pipelines Take a Hit." Although their business models are failing, our media corporations are as complicit in clinging to the status quo as our energy corporations, our miners and our logging companies. Seek no great truths from them.

Our governments? At the time of the Tŝilhqot'in decision, Prime Minister Stephen Harper was leading a government that could not be trusted on a single important issue. B.C. Premier Christy Clark began suddenly scurrying around the north of the province convening what she referred to as "chief-to-chief" meetings with Indigenous leaders she had hitherto ignored.

Premier Clark's interpretation of the decision was that there was "some good stuff in the Supreme Court decision" that she thought provided certainty and could even help "reinvigorate the treaty process." But on whose terms? The government's, of course.

Alone among our public institutions, the Supreme Court managed to sustain a vision of a Canada that offers justice and recognizes Indigenous rights, and much of the credit for that can be laid at the feet of Madam Justice Beverley McLachlin.

It is one of the happier accidents of history that it was in 1989, the year the Tŝilhqot'in launched their case in the B.C. Supreme Court, that Beverley McLachlin was promoted from being chief justice of that court in order to take up an appointment to the Supreme Court of Canada, where she served until she retired in 2017. It was McLachlin, as chief justice of Canada, who wrote the 8–0 judgment in favour of the Tŝilhqot'in fully twenty-five years after the case launched.

U.S. Supreme Court Associate Justice Stephen Breyer once described someone with a rare clarity of thought as having a "moonlight mind," and he could well have been describing McLachlin.

Her court clarified many important issues for Canadians. On labour rights, the court found for the union after a Walmart in Quebec closed its doors when workers dared to organize; on privacy rights, the court said police need a warrant to access information stored with internet service providers; on sex work, it stood up for sex workers; on criminal justice, it curbed the Tories' overreach for mandatory minimum sentences; regarding its own composition, the court outright refused to be saddled with Stephen Harper's unqualified choice for the bench, Justice Marc Nadon.

And now this. In crafting the Tŝilhqot'in decision, Beverley McLachlin ended a journey the Tŝilhqot'in began before B.C. even existed. The decision gives the force of law to help Canadians come to terms with the fact that we are all People of the Blue Water now. Indeed, we always have been.

QUICK FACTS ABOUT THE CHILCOTIN

→ The Chilcotin is the largest intact grassland in the world, and it is also home to rare white pelicans, trumpeter swans, bears, lynx, wolves, mountain caribou, wild horses and Canada's largest population of bighorn sheep.

→ The Chilcotin River is one of the most challenging white-water rivers to raft in North America.

→ Highway 20 runs 454 kilometres from Bella Coola to Williams Lake, through the Chilcotin. Known as Freedom Road or the Last Frontier, 137 kilometres of the road were built by volunteers between 1953 and 1955 because the government refused to extend the road through the mountainous terrain. Volunteers started at opposite ends of the road with bulldozers and supplies purchased on credit.

XWÍSTEN

A Fraser Full of Fish No More?

COLLEEN KIMMETT

(2008)

THE SCENE AT BRIDGE RIVER RAPIDS on an August afternoon during the late summer sockeye run is timeless.

Dozens of men stand on the rocky outcrops at the river's edge, holding nets on long poles over the churning water.

The salmon, silver bullets of pure muscle, ascend these class-five rapids in leaps. It's a matter of timing and location to land a fish as it springs out of the froth and, hopefully, into the dip-net.

People who aren't fishing are working and relaxing in the shade of blue tarpaulins; at least two dozen of these temporary shelters line each bank of the river.

Between them are wooden racks on which thin pieces of filleted salmon flesh hang, drying in the convection-oven heat of the Fraser Canyon. Preserved this way, the meat will last for months.

This place is called Xwísten. Narrow rock ledges at the confluence of the Bridge River form a natural obstacle to fish, making this location one of the busiest First Nations fishing spots on the river. In this warm, dry climate, vegetation is low and sparse, characterized by bunchgrass, sagebrush and cacti.

I am here with the Sustainable Living Leadership Program, which receives funding from the Rivershed

Society of BC. Together, we have travelled most of the length of the Fraser River, a three-week journey from source to sea, to see first-hand how British Columbians live and work on the Fraser, and gain a better understanding of how people, land and rivers are connected.

A thousand years ago, Xwísten people would have spent summers on these same rocks where we've stopped now, going through the same rituals. But if predictions hold true about the decline of salmon stocks in the Fraser, this tradition will end. For some of the people who depend on salmon in their culture and diet, that's simply unthinkable. But others fear their grandchildren will never see the wild salmon migration at all.

Ask ten people how it came to be this way and you will get ten different answers. Sea lice, pollution, loss of habitat, rising water temperatures—some of these are clearly linked to human behaviours and some might be beyond our control. "Salmon are dying a death of a thousand cuts," one fishery officer told me.

What's increasingly evident, no matter the precise mechanism of the decline, is the need for a new system of managing this precarious resource.

CHICO WILLIAMS, the ferry operator at Big Bar crossing, about sixty kilometres north of Lillooet in the Fraser Canyon, says the solution to recover fish stocks is simple: stop fishing, at least for a little while.

Williams, a short, stocky man with slicked-back hair and tattoos up both muscled forearms, worked on commercial trawlers in the North Pacific in the 1970s, at a time when the oceans' fisheries seemed inexhaustible.

In those days, says Williams, migrating sockeye would be so thick on the Fraser you could walk across the river without getting your feet wet.

Now he sees so few he's given up fishing at all. "It's just common sense," he says. "I want my grandkids to be able to fish."

Sharolise Baker shares this view. She is the fisheries manager for the Stellat'en First Nation near Fraser Lake, where last year very few sockeye were caught in the community fish weir, which forces fish to one side of the river where they are harvested or allowed through.

Amidst predictions of the lowest-ever Fraser sockeye return, Baker raised the possibility of a total moratorium on sockeye at a meeting with fishery officers and various First Nations fisheries managers.

"The room got pretty darn quiet," she says. Yet, in her opinion, drastic conservation measures have to be taken. "We should be saying no to everybody. Commercial, sport and First Nations."

The Stellat'en are "last in line" to have access to the fish, Baker says. Until there is a moratorium on all sockeye fishing in the entire migration corridor, she isn't going to ask her own people to let them swim by.

"First Nations, particularly further upstream in the natal areas, rely on very few stocks because they fish close to home," says Neil Todd of the Fraser River Aboriginal Fisheries Secretariat.

"So they have access to far fewer stocks than people who fish in the main stem. This has been an issue for fifty, one hundred years."

Although fisheries managers inside and outside Fisheries and Oceans Canada "understand and accept it can't be an exact science," says Todd, both the uncertainty of salmon run estimates, and the allocation of commercial and recreational rights based on those estimates, are a point of contention for many First Nations.

The underlying issue, Todd says, is the fact that B.C.'s commercial fishery is a mixed-stock fishery. It happens in the marine areas, where strong and weak stocks mingle before heading up the river to their respective spawning grounds.

In these marine areas, there's no way to tell if a salmon is from a stock with very weak or fairly healthy numbers. So certain stocks, Cultus Lake sockeye for example, face a very real risk of complete extinction.

Sockeye salmon stocks have been in decline for over a century, and some of the most critically endangered runs are in British Columbia.

Mike Griswold, vice-president of the Gulf Trollers Association, says the government should compensate commercial fishermen for taking their boats off the water.

"There has been a massive reduction in harvest but the fleet has stayed the same, so what's left for us to harvest has been minimal," he says. "Quite a few of us are going bankrupt."

PORTAGING THROUGH the Bridge River fishing grounds, we pause briefly to chat with a young man coming up from the water. He's bent over from the weight of a big backpack lined with a garbage bag.

Fishing's been good, he tells us. He's caught fifteen today and will come back for more later. Fifty-three is the most any one person has caught this season, he says, and the "springers" are landing in dip-nets two and three at a time.

I ask if he's worried about taking too many. "No," he says. "There's lots."

One of our participants from Fraser Lake, who signed up for the program at Baker's urging, is taken aback by the number of people here and the volume of red flesh strung up to dry.

"They're taking so many," she says. To someone from a community where salmon are scarce, this seems excessive. But six different bands from the area come here to fish, someone points out.

Driving through Soda Creek in the pouring rain one evening, we stumble across Xatśūll Heritage Village. Owned and operated by the Xatśūll First Nation, the site is a grassy plateau on a tall cliff overlooking the river (*Xatśūll* means "on the cliff").

Like children, we run for a semicircle of teepees that will be our shelter tonight and start exploring the site. I meet Jordell Sellars and Fallon Williams, two Xatśūll First Nation members who are here to monitor the catch.

The salmon mean everything to her people, Williams tells me. When her grandmother is sick, she eats nothing but salmon-head soup.

I ask how they pick the fishing spots and Williams pauses a moment, thinking. They've just always been there, she says. Since forever.

QUICK FACTS ABOUT XWÍSTEN

→ *Xwísten* means "smiling people" in the language of the St'át'imc Nation.

→ The remains of Xwísten pithouses, which were winter dwellings, have been found to date back 1,800 years. The houses were deep pits in the ground, built upwards via large upright posts and covered with matting. Up to four families could live in one pithouse.

→ Before B.C. built the Terzaghi Dam in the 1950s, the Bridge River salmon run was one of the world's largest. The Xwísten relied on salmon for seventy percent of the protein in their diet.

ACKNOWLEDGEMENTS

"The Great Arrow Creek Disaster," by Dorothy Woodend, is adapted from "I've Finally Decided to Learn How to Drive. Hop In," published on The Tyee on December 9, 2019.

"Newcomers to Doukhobor Territory," by Leesa Dean, was published on The Tyee on February 3, 2023.

"'Everything Is Burning and Your House Is Gone,'" by Michelle Gamage, was published on The Tyee on December 14, 2021.

"To Honour the Lost, a Cattle Drive," by Kate Helmore, was originally published on The Tyee as a photo essay, "To Honour the Lost, a Cattle Drive in the Osoyoos Desert," on June 28, 2022.

"The Art of Growing Wheat in the Rain," by Christopher Cheung, is adapted from "Growing Wheat Is a Rare Art in Rainy B.C. Meet Some Pioneers," published on The Tyee on June 30, 2020.

"The Blacker the Berry," by Harrison Mooney, was commissioned for publication in this book.

"Tending the Fields of Resistance," by David P. Ball, is adapted from "Charan Gill: An 'Epic' Life of Advocacy," published on The Tyee on February 7, 2021.

"Amidst the Tourists, Creating a 'Landscape of Fear,'" by Michelle Cyca, is adapted from "A Week in the Life: A Falconer at YVR and Granville Island," published on The Tyee on September 8, 2022.

"Elegy for a Building Manager," by Steve Burgess, was originally published on The Tyee as "Elegy for My Building Manager" on December 17, 2020.

"Dumplings for a New Year," by Fiona Tinwei Lam, was originally published on The Tyee as "Rolling Dumplings With Mom" on January 31, 2014.

"The Golden Village at the Edge of the Ocean," by Christopher Cheung, is adapted from "'Ethnoburbs': The New Face of Immigrant Cities," published on The Tyee on August 5, 2016; "No Return Ticket," published on June 30, 2022; "Goodbye to a Tai Chi Master at a Richmond Mall," published on August 12, 2022; and "Overrun With Buns," published on January 27, 2023.

"A Beachcomber's Love Story," by Abi Hayward, was published on The Tyee on September 10, 2019.

"A Wild and Woolly Issue," by andrea bennett, was originally published on The Tyee as "On Lasqueti Island, a Wild and Woolly Issue Has Divided Residents" on September 23, 2021.

"The Worst Windstorm in BC Hydro's History," by Sofia Osborne, was originally published on The Tyee as "Dad's World Was My Refuge, Until the Wind Storm Hit" on January 28, 2019.

"How I Salvaged My Sense of Wonder," by Tim B. Rogers, is adapted from "Trained in Dispassion, Here's How I Salvaged My Sense of Wonder," published on The Tyee on September 2, 2022.

"More *Deadwood* Than *Downton Abbey*," by Tom Hawthorn, was commissioned for publication in this book.

"Three Days in the Theatre of an Old-Growth Blockade," by Arno Kopecky, was produced in collaboration with Hakai Magazine and was first published as "Three Days in the Theatre of Fairy Creek" on The Tyee on June 1, 2021.

"'Residential School Perverted Everything That Was Beautiful,'" by Meghan Mast, was originally published on The Tyee as "Still Surviving: Reconciliation Through Everyday Rebellion" on June 2, 2015, and then updated for republication as "'Residential School Perverted Everything That Was Beautiful'" on July 19, 2021.

"'This Is Homecoming,'" by Michael John Lo, was originally published on The Tyee as "Cumberland's Chinese Heart" on August 11, 2022.

"Fishing in the Haig-Brown Library," by Andrew Nikiforuk, was published on The Tyee on May 31, 2014.

"When a Trip to the Post Office Takes Half a Day," by Karen Charleson, was originally published on The Tyee as "Picking Up the Mail: Life on the Wild West Coast" on December 16, 2019.

"At Canada's End of the Road," by Ben Mussett, was originally published on The Tyee as "At Canada's End of the Road, a Visit With Anne Cameron" on May 8, 2020, and then updated and republished after Cameron's November 30, 2022, death, on December 7, 2022.

"The Riddle of the Monkey Puzzle Tree," by Neil Griffin, was published on The Tyee on November 4, 2022.

"Winter Is for Regeneration," by 'Cúagilákv (Jess H̓áust̓i) was originally published on The Tyee as "Winter Is for Regeneration. The Garden's—and Yours, Too" on December 14, 2021.

"Serving the Cranberry Crowd," by Fiona McGlynn, was published on The Tyee on February 9, 2023.

"All A'bored the Skeena Train," by Amanda Follett Hosgood, was originally published on The Tyee as "All A'bored: Riding the Sweet, but So Slow, Skeena Train" on July 17, 2019.

"The 100-Mile Diet Goes North," by J. B. MacKinnon and Alisa Smith, was published on The Tyee on August 23, 2005.

"The World's Most Remote Brewery?" by Amanda Follett Hosgood, was published on The Tyee on July 20, 2022.

"To the Tŝilhqot'in, With Gloves," by Ian Gill, was published on The Tyee on July 26, 2014.

"A Fraser Full of Fish No More?" by Colleen Kimmett, was published on The Tyee on December 3, 2008.

CONTRIBUTORS

DAVID P. BALL has been a multimedia journalist for more than twenty years, contributing to The Tyee since 2011. Based in Vancouver, he has also reported for Agence France-Presse and the *Toronto Star,* and has appeared in the *Globe and Mail,* the *Times of India,* the *Guardian* and *Vice,* and in public radio and podcasting. David has won awards from the Canadian Association of Journalists, the Jack Webster Foundation and the Canadian Journalism Foundation. In his free time, he plays flute and forages for fungi, flora and fauna.

ANDREA BENNETT is a National Magazine Award–winning writer and senior editor at The Tyee. They are the author of five books, including *Like a Boy but Not a Boy,* a CBC Books pick for top Canadian non-fiction of 2020. Their next book, *Hearty: Essays on Pleasure and Subsistence,* is forthcoming from ECW Press.

STEVE BURGESS is a contributing editor at The Tyee and author of the 2011 book *Who Killed Mom?* from Greystone Books. He has won two National Magazine Awards and three Western Magazine Awards, and received the City Mike Award at the 2023 Websters for his work with The Tyee. His new book, *Flight Risk: A Tourist on Trial,* will be published by Harbour Publishing in spring 2024.

KAREN CHARLESON is a mother, grandmother, educator and writer. Through marriage, Karen is a member of the Hesquiaht First Nation and the House of Kinquashtakumlth. She lives in Hesquiaht traditional territories on the west coast of Vancouver Island.

CHRISTOPHER CHEUNG is a Vancouver journalist who has written for The Tyee since 2015. His wide-ranging urban-issues beat has led him to report on everything from the gentrification of the city, East Asian malls in suburbia, and food factories that make cultural staples like tofu, tortillas and Indian dairy.

ʼCÚAGILÁKV (JESS H̓ÁUST̓I) is a Haíłzaqv parent, writer and land-based educator from the community of Bella Bella, B.C. They live in their unceded ancestral homelands, where they work in community building, food sovereignty and leadership development.

MICHELLE CYCA is a freelance journalist and editor. Her features, essays and literary criticism can be found in the *Walrus*, *Chatelaine*, the *Globe and Mail*, *IndigiNews* and The Tyee, among other publications. She is a lifelong Vancouverite and unofficial global ambassador for the city's distinctive beach logs.

LEESA DEAN (she/her) is a graduate of the University of Guelph's creative writing MFA program and teaches creative writing at Selkirk College. She is the author of *Waiting for the Cyclone* (2016), *The Desert of Itabira* (2020), *The Filling Station* (2022) and *Apogee/Perigee* (forthcoming). She is a settler in the unceded territory of the Sinixt in Krestova, B.C.

AMANDA FOLLETT HOSGOOD is The Tyee's northern B.C. reporter. Born and raised in Ontario, she began her journalism career more than twenty years ago at community newspapers in Alberta, before freelancing for publications like *British Columbia Magazine*, *Coast Mountain Culture* and *Explore* magazine. She lives with her family just outside Smithers, B.C.

MICHELLE GAMAGE is The Tyee's health reporter. She previously wrote about environmental and climate change issues for the magazine. Her work earned her the Digital Publishing Awards' Emerging Excellence Award in 2022.

IAN GILL is an Australian-born author, journalist, critic, conservationist and co-founder of the west coast bioregional initiative Salmon Nation. He chairs its non-profit arm, Magic Canoe. Ian worked for almost twenty years as CEO of Ecotrust in Canada, the U.S. and Australia, and has extensive experience in community and economic development in coastal communities along North America's west coast. He is co-founder of Upstart & Crow, a bookstore and literary arts studio on Vancouver's Granville Island, and is a contributing editor at The Tyee. His book on Haida Gwaii, *All That We Say Is Ours*, was re-released in paperback in 2022.

NEIL GRIFFIN is an award-winning poet, essayist and naturalist. More of his work is available at neilcgriffin.com.

TOM HAWTHORN, who has lived in Victoria for more than twenty-five years, has been a contributor to The Tyee since 2004. He is the author of two books. A veteran newspaper and magazine journalist, he has been a speechwriter for two B.C. premiers.

ABI HAYWARD is a writer, editor and ocean nerd. After several years reporting in Vancouver—having moved to Canada from Yorkshire—she now happily dwells among the lakes and rivers of Ottawa, where she is the associate editor at *Canadian Geographic*. She loves maps, sea sponges, her cats and her partner.

KATE HELMORE is a freelance journalist based in Vancouver. Her features, photography and essays can be found in The Tyee, the *Globe and Mail* and *Canadian Geographic*, among other publications. Although born in the United Kingdom, Kate is drawn to the landscape of British Columbia and the stories that it holds.

NORA KELLY, whose illustrations run through this book, is a visual artist and musician who grew up in Vancouver and now lives in Montreal.

COLLEEN KIMMETT is a writer who lives in Montreal. She has worked as a reporter, editor, writing coach and newsroom trainer. Colleen loves to spend her free time exploring wild swimming spots.

ARNO KOPECKY is an award-winning environmental journalist and author who has been contributing to The Tyee since 2009. He lives with his wife and daughter in Vancouver.

FIONA TINWEI LAM, Vancouver's sixth poet laureate, has authored three poetry collections and a children's book. Her work is featured in over forty-five anthologies, including *Best Canadian Poetry*, and in award-winning collaborative poetry videos. She edited *The Bright Well: Contemporary Canadian Poems about Facing Cancer*, and co-edited two non-fiction anthologies. fionalam.net.

MICHAEL JOHN LO is a journalist based in Victoria and Vancouver. He got his start at the University of Victoria's student paper, the *Martlet*, and has been reporting on B.C. stories ever since. One of his dreams is to eat at every ramen shop inside Metro Vancouver.

J. B. MACKINNON and ALISA SMITH co-wrote *The 100-Mile Diet* (2007), widely recognized as a catalyst of the local foods movement. Smith is also author of the novels *Speakeasy* and *Doublespeak*; MacKinnon's most recent book is *The Day the World Stops Shopping*. Smith and MacKinnon live in Vancouver.

MEGHAN MAST is a freelance writer and radio producer living in Treaty 1 territory, Winnipeg, the original land of the Anishinaabe, Cree and Dakota peoples, and the homeland of the Métis Nation. She produced a radio documentary about Gina Laing and Dennis Bob for CBC Radio's *The Doc Project* in 2022.

FIONA MCGLYNN moved to Atlin, B.C., in 2018 after spending three years sailing from Canada to Australia on a thirty-five-foot boat with her husband, Robin. She's won several awards for her boating writing and has contributed to the *Globe and Mail*, *Cottage Life* and *Canadian Geographic*, among others. She also started WaterborneMag.com to help people launch their own sailing adventures.

HARRISON MOONEY is an award-winning author and journalist from the Fraser Valley. His debut memoir, *Invisible Boy: A Memoir of Self-Discovery*, has been shortlisted for the Kobo Emerging Writer Prize, as well as two BC and Yukon Book Prizes, and was named a *Globe and Mail* and CBC best book of 2022. Mooney's essays have also appeared in the *Vancouver Sun*, the *Guardian* and *Maclean's*. He lives in East Vancouver with his family.

BEN MUSSETT is a British Columbia–born writer who now lives in Toronto with his partner and an inscrutable orange cat. His work has appeared in the *Toronto Star*, the *Globe and Mail*, *Vice News*, Capital Daily and, of course, The Tyee.

ANDREW NIKIFORUK has written about the abuse of natural resources in Canada for more than thirty-five years. His books include *Slick Water*, *Tar Sands*, *Empire of the Beetle*, *The Energy of Slaves* and *Pandemonium*.

SOFIA OSBORNE is a freelance writer, editor and audio producer, currently completing her MFA in creative writing at the University of British Columbia. Her writing on the environment and identity has appeared in The Tyee, *Maisonneuve*, the Narwhal and *This Magazine*.

TIM B. ROGERS is a writer, photographer and musician who lives in Victoria, B.C. He is a former University of Calgary professor and social scientist. With his faithful Labrador retriever, Skipper, he frequents the woodlands near his home on the lookout for anything interesting or unusual, and takes advantage of the many photo ops offered up by this magical place.

DOROTHY WOODEND started writing for The Tyee in 2004 and simply never stopped. In addition to covering culture, she has worked with a number of different arts organizations, including DOXA Documentary Film Festival, the Vancouver International Film Festival and the National Film Board of Canada. In her spare time, she draws a lot of frogs.